Listening
to the Experts

Listening to the Experts

Students with Disabilities Speak Out

edited by

Elizabeth B. Keefe, Ph.D.

Veronica M. Moore, Ph.D.

and

Frances R. Duff, M.A.

·P A U L·H·
BROOKES
PUBLISHING CO®

Baltimore • London • Sydney

Paul H. Brookes Publishing Co.
Post Office Box 10624
Baltimore, Maryland 21285-0624

www.brookespublishing.com

"Paul H. Brookes Publishing Co." is a registered trademark of
Paul H. Brookes Publishing Co., Inc.

Typeset by International Graphic Services of New Jersey, Inc., Newtown,
Pennsylvania.
Manufactured in the United States of America by
Versa Press, Inc., East Peoria, Illinois.

The stories in this book refer to real-life experiences. Many of the
individuals' names and other identifying features have been changed to
protect individuals' identities. Stories involving real names and details
are used by permission.

Individuals featured in the stories have kindly granted permission for
their photographs to be used.

Photographs on pages 53 and 141 courtesy of Kim Jew Photography.

Library of Congress Cataloging-in-Publication Data

Listening to the experts : students with disabilities speak out / edited by
   Elizabeth B. Keefe, Veronica M. Moore, and Frances R. Duff.
     p.   cm.
   Includes bibliographical references and index.
   ISBN-13: 978-1-55766-836-3 (pbk.)
   ISBN-10: 1-55766-836-1 (pbk.)
   1. Students with disabilities—United States   2. High school
   students—United States   3. Mainstreaming in education—United
   States.   I. Keefe, Elizabeth B.   II. Moore, Veronica M.   III. Duff,
   Frances R.
   LC4015.L57   2006
   371.9092'2—dc22   2005035724

British Library Cataloguing in Publication data are available from the
British Library.

Contents

About the Editors

Elizabeth B. Keefe, Ph.D., Associate Professor, Department of Educational Specialties, University of New Mexico, Albuquerque, New Mexico 87131

Dr. Keefe received her bachelor's degree in sociology from the University of Newcastle-upon-Tyne in the United Kingdom, her master's degree in anthropology at the University of Nebraska, and her master of arts and doctoral degrees in special education from the University of New Mexico. She has taught in inclusive settings at the elementary level and now is actively involved in various educational reform issues throughout New Mexico. Her research interests include inclusive practices, co-teaching, and systemic change at the school level. Dr. Keefe enjoys tennis, playing banjo with her band, going to Jamaica, and reading.

Veronica M. Moore, Ph.D., Lecturer, Department of Educational Specialties, University of New Mexico, Albuquerque, New Mexico 87131

Dr. Moore co-coordinates the dual license teacher preparation program at the University of New Mexico. She received her bachelor of arts degree in English and her master of arts and doctoral degrees in special education at the University of New Mexico. In addition to teaching at the University of New Mexico, Dr. Moore co-teaches an inclusive class one period per day at the high school level. Her research interests include peer supports, student voice, inclusive practices, and curriculum modifications. She enjoys traveling, playing tennis, and gardening.

Frances R. Duff, M.A., Teacher, Language Arts and Humanities, Cibola High School, 1510 Ellison NW, Albuquerque, New Mexico 87114

Ms. Duff is a National Board Certified Teacher with more than 25 years of experience in the classroom. She earned her bachelor's degree in psychology from New York University and her master's degree in special education from the University of New Mexico. She is currently pursuing her doctoral degree at the University of New Mexico. Ms. Duff has worked with various grade levels in New York, California, and New Mexico. She currently co-teaches three inclusive classes at the high school level. Her research interests are inclusive practices, legal issues, and advocacy and empowerment for students. Ms. Duff enjoys reading and playing with the family dog, Bear.

Despite their hectic schedules, all of the editors cherish the time they get to spend with their families. They work extensively in the public schools to support teachers, students, and families. The editors enjoy collaborating with classroom teachers, students, administrators, and family members to co-present at local, national, and international conferences. This book represents an important step in the editors' goal of making sure that families and students with disabilities are equal partners in scholarship.

Contributors

Stanley Agustin, M.A.
Ginger Blalock, Ph.D.
Eddie Castro
Phillip Contreras
Susan R. Copeland, Ph.D.
Heather Curran
Douglas Fisher, Ph.D.
Amanda Funicelli
Angela Gabel
Amanda Goshorn
Bea Etta Harris, Ed.D.
Gary Hartzog
Farrah Hernton
Kathryn Herr, Ph.D.
Kelsey Holmes

Erin Jarry, M.A.
Sherry Jones, M.S.
Ruth Luckasson, J.D.
Jeremy Mallak
Carolyn Metzler, M.A.
Michelle Murray
Breanna Ortiz
Stacey Pearson
Erin Pitcher
Carson Proo
Victor Proo
Chad Schrimpf
Elliott Shelton
Katherine Shelton
Alex Weatherhead

Foreword
Thinking About Experts and Expertise

In our multitasking society today, it is not uncommon for people to read more than one book at a time. Such was the case when I was invited to write the foreword for an exciting new book by Elizabeth B. Keefe, Veronica M. Moore, and Frances R. Duff. I had just started *Blink: The Power of Thinking without Thinking* by Malcolm Gladwell (2005) as part of a book club that I'm in when I received a copy of *Listening to the Experts: Students with Disabilities Speak Out* to review.

If we are fortunate, our worlds collide, and we make connections between what we know, what we are reading, and our experiences. This is exactly what happened as I read these two books. Given that you, my reader, are likely to have more experience with schooling, disability, and young people, I'll start with a discussion about *Blink* and then make connections between the ideas that Gladwell posited and the experiences Keefe, Moore, and Duff share.

Gladwell made the case that we can, and in fact we do, quickly size up situations and make decisions. In other words, contrary to the popular sentiment, first impressions do matter, and we don't always need to spend a lot of time "looking before we leap." He called this *rapid cognition* and believes it is part of being human. We use small bits of information, often recognized by our adaptive unconscious, to "thin-slice" a situation and make a decision. One of the many examples he shared focused on a psychologist who can listen to a married couple discuss something from their life and determine, within 15 minutes and with 95% accuracy, if they will be divorced within the next 15 years. Gladwell also described hiring practices of the Munich Philharmonic, which had virtually no women players until they used a "blind" review process in which the judges and interview committee could not see the applicant.

These two brief examples highlight some important ideas about expertise. First, experts can make very rapid decisions that are accurate. As Gladwell pointed out, with training and experience, experts can make rapid decisions and hit their target with significant accuracy. He cited numerous examples of athletes, generals, police officers, and physicians who use their "adaptive unconscious" to thin-slice a situation and make a very good decision.

Gladwell also pointed out that experts are fallible, that they sometimes allow their prejudices and stereotypes to interfere with their ability to thin-slice and use rapid cognition. Such was the case, as Gladwell noted, of the police killing of an unarmed immigrant Amadou Diallo in the Bronx in 1999. Diallo was on his stoop after midnight and didn't appear afraid of the police. Following a series of decisions and judgments, the police fired 41 shots and ended this man's life.

So what does this have to do with *Listening to the Experts?* I would argue, a great deal. First, Keefe, Moore, and Duff challenge us to think about what it means to be an expert and to have expertise. They purposefully shift our concept of expert and expand it to include a range of stakeholders within the educational enterprise. They intentionally collected the stories and experiences of students and identified students' areas of expertise. They also collected the experiences of parents and gave voice to these members of the educational community.

You should know that this is rare. While there are examples of family members' expertise being shared with the larger educational establishment (e.g., Erwin & Soodak, 1995), the voices of students with disabilities have been significantly absent from the professional literature. When students without disabilities are invited to share their thinking about students with disabilities and inclusive schooling, they often discuss human rights issues (e.g., Fisher, 1999). Can we say the same about students with disabilities? Until now, it has been very hard to find credible sources of expertise from students with disabilities. Keefe, Moore, and Duff have assumed the responsibility of changing our definition of expert and have shared this expertise with us.

But wait—there's more. As Gladwell pointed out, experts can be wrong. They can allow their stereotypes and biases to interfere with their judgments and decisions. So, what's the solution? Can we change these biases? Can we undo the conditioning that leads us to make poor decisions, decisions that are based on outdated information and ideas?

Gladwell noted that we can. His case in point is a person who wants to change his beliefs about people of color. This person tests himself daily on a reaction scale designed to determine the implicit associations he made about African Americans (for information on

this assessment, see http://implicit.harvard.edu/implicit/demo/
selectatest.html; there is also an Implicit Association Test related
to disability on this web site). This person was not able to change
his "slight preference for white people" despite many attempts at
the test until one morning when he took the test after watching the
Olympics. As Gladwell noted, watching the Olympics served to
"prime" his reaction and thus changed his thinking about people of
color. While this may have been a temporary situation, Gladwell
argued that over time we can change our responses to situations by
teaching our adaptive unconscious.

This is exactly what Keefe, Moore, and Duff have done. *Listening
to the Experts* serves to prime readers to consider and value the
perspectives of students with disabilities as they make decisions
that affect lives. As such, readers should read and reread these stories
on a regular basis. In this way, we will begin to make decisions with
and for students with disabilities that clearly demonstrate that we
value them, their families, their lives, their choices, and their rights
to be full, active members of our inclusive, diverse, and wonderful
world. I can't say this enough—this book should hold a valued place
on our desks (perhaps with a second copy next to our beds?) so that
we can regularly prime ourselves to consider who the system is for
as we go about our daily tasks of providing an exceptional, inclusive,
and individualized educational experience for each of our students.

Douglas Fisher, Ph.D.
Professor of Teacher Education
San Diego State University

REFERENCES

Erwin, E.J., & Soodak, L.C. (1995). I never knew I could stand up to the
system: Families' perspectives on pursuing inclusive education. *Journal
of The Association for Persons with Severe Handicaps, 20,* 136–146.

Fisher, D. (1999). According to their peers: Inclusion as high school students
see it. *Mental Retardation, 37,* 458–467.

Gladwell, M. (2005). *Blink: The power of thinking without thinking.* New
York: Little, Brown.

Acknowledgments

There are several individuals and organizations who deserve our appreciation and recognition for their role in supporting our efforts in producing this book. Among them is the New Mexico Public Education Department for their partial financial support to the writing and editing of this book. Rich Villa, Douglas Fisher, and Sam Howarth have provided inspiration with their unceasing work and dedication to realizing a vision of a world where all people belong. We are grateful to Grace Brown, Elena Salazar, and Amy Owens for their leadership, friendship, and support throughout this process. We owe much to the parents who have allowed us to work with their children and continue to entrust us daily to educate them.

The core of our efforts has been supported and energized by our students, whose words give voice to the reality of education in our country. We especially want to recognize Amber Sanchez as a charter member of the first peer buddies class at her school. We also want to thank Ryan Kennedy, Audrey Sanchez, Brittany Sanchez, and their classmates for showing us the possibilities of open minds and open hearts.

There are countless others who have contributed to this book by offering support or resources when we needed them. Some of these people are Linda Sink; Nancy Lacher; New Mexico Least Restrictive Environment (LRE) Core and Planning Teams; Evonne Sanchez; Julio "Dee" Magaña; Elizabeth Cochrane; Kate Orloff; Chris Sylvan; Katie Slimak; and Danny, Lesley, Jeff, and Karen Lederer. We would like to thank Rebecca Lazo, Steve Peterson, and Janet Betten at Paul H. Brookes Publishing Co. for their work in making our book a reality.

Special recognition is owed to Charlotte Mullins for her work as a pioneer in inclusive education in the state of New Mexico. She lit fires and enlightened all of us to begin and continue our work in educating *all* students in the least restrictive environment.

To our wonderful families
Mike, Andrew, and Meg Keefe
George and Mavis Barker
Michael, Katie, and Kyle Moore
Carol and Matthew O'Nuska
Asa and Cristin Duff

Thank you for your never-ending patience and support.

Introduction
Breaking the Silence

This is not a book about special education. It is not an admonition to comply with special education law, nor is it an impassioned plea for social justice. This is a book about possibilities. This is a testament to the strength of the human spirit. The chapters document the tenacity of students who have battled against the odds in a world that often does not hear them. This is a glimpse into the lives of high school students and a chance to hear their own experiences in their own words.

It is clear that the power of this book lies in the honesty of the students. They speak openly of successes, failures, heartaches, and fears. Ultimately they triumphed, often in spite of a system that seemed to prevent them from being heard. Sadly, most students' voices are drowned out by the bureaucracy and pressures of educational systems. It is time to break the silence.

We were strongly influenced in our quest by Pano Rodis, Andrew Garrod, and Mary Lynn Boscardin's (2001) anthology of student voices, *Learning Disabilities and Life Stories*. Their work helped us to revise our teaching practices and to learn to listen to the innate expertise of our students. After reading the anthology's accounts of adults with learning disabilities as they reflected on their high school years, we were eager to hear from high school students themselves. We collected these stories over a 3-year period from high school students who were invited to write chapters for this book. We asked them, "Tell us about school. What is it like for you?" Their responses are heartfelt and frank. Their eloquence exists in their candor. It provides a whole new understanding of the day-to-day struggle to survive and flourish in high school.

The relationships that develop in high school represent the social stratification inherent in society as a whole. According to Wexler (1992), the interactions that take place between students in high school are predictors of broader fundamental social issues. Given the fact that many typical students are not given opportunities to develop relationships with students with disabilities, what are these high school students learning about the human rights of individuals with disabilities?

In Chapter 3, Ruth Luckasson shows us how the school experience is a crucial element in preparing individuals to exercise their basic human rights, and this leads to deeper learning and education. In Chapter 30, Kelsey Holmes reminds us that no one should be denied the basic human need to belong. She echoes the belief that school is a microcosm of society, and developing relationships with diverse individuals is the only way to create an equitable world. In Chapters 9 and 10, Farrah Hernton and Michelle Murray tell the story of how difficult it can be sometimes just to exercise the right to have lunch with your friends.

The need to include students with disabilities and their typical peers in all facets of the school experience is not just an exercise in social justice; it is also embedded in the law. The Individuals with Disabilities Education Improvement Act of 2004 (IDEA 2004; PL 108-446) is clear about the rights of individuals who receive special education services in its statement that

> Disability is a natural part of the human experience and in no way diminishes the right of individuals to participate or contribute to society. Improving educational results for children with disabilities is an essential element of our national policy of ensuring equality of opportunity, full participation, independent living and economic self sufficiency for individuals with disabilities. (IDEA 2004, § 601 [c][1])

The law, both in letter and spirit, clearly indicates that individuals with disabilities have the same human rights as those without disabilities. One would assume that allowing students with disabilities opportunities to collaborate with teachers or school officials would be a valued contribution to the field; however, as demonstrated by Veronica M. Moore (Chapter 4), the limited research base in this area indicates that student voice has not been taken seriously. Why listen to student voices? Students are directly affected by what professionals promote as being "best practices." Whether or not these practices are truly "best" can only be determined in collaboration with the students who are directly affected. Based on our review of existing literature, we believe this is an area of the research that is sorely lacking, and we hope that the insight provided from our chapter contributors can create a greater awareness of the importance of student perspectives, especially when creating environments that welcome and acknowledge the strengths of all members of the community.

Why is it important to create inclusive schools? We need look no further than IDEA 2004, where Congress noted,

Almost 30 years of research and experience has demonstrated that the education of children with disabilities can be made more effective by having high expectations for such children and ensuring their access to the general education curriculum in the regular classroom to the maximum extent possible. (§ 601 [c] [5])

Congress clearly envisioned that students with and without disabilities should have the opportunity to be educated together. This book is a valuable addition to the literature on inclusive education by communicating the reality of inclusive and segregated settings on students with and without disabilities from their perspective based on real experiences. Listen to the voices of the students in this book as they bring the letter and spirit of IDEA 2004 to life. Chapter 12, by Erin Pitcher, is a particularly moving example of the positive consequences that can result for students without disabilities from their friendship with peers with severe disabilities.

How do we create inclusive classrooms? There are many research articles and "how to" books on inclusive education. This book offers professional perspectives on practices that we believe to be among the most effective in reaching high school students—collaboration and coteaching, peer collaboration, and differentiated instruction—however, actual practice in the field reaches beyond a theoretical framework and into the daily lives of our students. What looks good in the text of an article or in the results of an inquiry finds its true value when it touches the lives of students in the day-to-day world of a typical high school.

Scholars and authors, including some in this book, write about techniques and strategies that have been effective in classroom practice. Their work is based on sound research and years of practical experience; however, the effectiveness of their methods is viewed through a scholarly lens. The reality of the classroom challenges each teacher to evaluate the practical value of practices that are labeled *best* by scholars and to determine if that label holds true for individual students. Regardless of data collected by universities and government departments, the true expert on learning is the learner. The student authors tell us in their own words what practices really were *best* for them in their classrooms and schools. They do not offer us advice; they merely tell us of their experiences and allow us to see ourselves in their eyes. They offer us the data collected in their hearts and trust us to live up to their expectations.

What supports are needed for schools to really change? We believe that above all administrative leadership is critical. Chapter 17, by Stanley Agustin and Elizabeth B. Keefe, tells the story of a restructured school that both belongs to the students and is a place where students belong. The principal and staff have embraced the vision of inclusive education for all students. This chapter demonstrates how the Circle of Courage (Van Bockern, Brendtro, & Brokenleg, 2000) can provide a framework for schools who truly embrace the idea that all children can learn together. Another principal, Bea Etta Harris, in Chapter 26 tells the very personal story of her journey as the leader of a school restructuring for inclusive education. These administrators show how strong leadership can result in real and lasting change for students and educators.

We cannot be concerned only about what happens to students in our schools. We also need to ask what happens to our students after graduation. The process of transition begins early in a student's school experiences. As we move our students from grade to grade and from school to school, we offer them insight into the process of decision making. We guide them in evaluating outcomes and preparing for the next step. As students mature and become more sophisticated in their knowledge of the system, more decisions should rest on their shoulders. Ginger Blalock, in Chapter 28, reminds the adults in the transition process that the command base of decisions ultimately must transfer to the students themselves.

Transition planning should not merely present information about facilities and services available to students but also should help students create and reinforce their own bridges to the next phase of their lives in school and beyond. The ultimate goal of transition is to prepare students for the rest of their lives. We need to help them build their own arsenal of skills and abilities to achieve their dreams for themselves. We cannot be satisfied with the world as it is if it does not meet the demands of justice and equity that our children deserve.

Do we see our students as advocates? Have we empowered them? The answer to both questions is a qualified yes—some students, sometimes. Our failures are quickly evident when we see schools that continue to segregate according to label and/or perceived ability or when we see graduates scrambling to find a way to escape the dependence on others that our system has fostered in them. We observe failure in the making when we hear the voice of our children pointing out the inequity in their education. For example, Elliott Shelton, in Chapter 1, tells us clearly where the system let him down and even informs us of strategies that would have benefited him if we had tried. It is apparent that support outside the educational hierarchy allowed Elliott to succeed. There are lessons to be learned from his eloquent description of his struggle to learn.

Chapters by many of the students tell the story of the challenges they faced and overcame. Sometimes their success was bolstered by teachers who heard their voices; sometimes they relied on fellow students to help them overcome institutional obstacles. What these students offer us is the opportunity to begin building success for all of our students by listening to their voices now, while change can still be effected in our schools. These students have long been talking to us; it's time now to hear them.

What kind of a world do we all want to live in? What kinds of educators do we want to be? This book contains the perspectives of professionals who have focused their careers on improving educational outcomes for children. These instructional leaders are visionaries who believe in the power of student voice and have a philosophical commitment to include and involve all students in the learning process. A number of chapters are written by school administrators and classroom teachers who are leading their schools in responding to the voices of the students. These educators have changed their teaching practices because of transformational experiences with children. Other contributors include disability advocates and researchers who diligently investigate the needs of students and transform their findings into effective support systems for individuals who have been denied a "fair shot" at education. We are grateful to these individuals for the talent and insight they have added to this topic.

Regardless of the talent or dedication of teachers or administrators, it is impossible to comprehend the reality of the high school experience without help from the students, the true experts in education. Although these student accounts do not resemble typical professional perspectives, their significance should not be discounted. These are, in fact, substantial contributions to our field that provide an insight that the traditional literature has never been able to fully address. The student authors' experiences are immediate. They are not retrospective accounts tempered by wisdom and the distance of years.

Moreover, these chapters are composed entirely by the students, with only minimal editorial assistance. Their remarks are not filtered through any theoretical lens. We provide no thematic analyses or academic bent to their words. The stories are pure so that you can hear what we heard, as our students became our mentors. They inform us of how our roles need to evolve in order to become the teachers children really need.

We offer no judgments or interpretations but merely open a door into the students' world. We hope you will absorb the power of the messages as they come straight from the hearts of these young men and women. When you embrace the lessons inherent in these stories, we believe you will change your teaching practice forever.

Ultimately, we have the power to change the system that has both encouraged and hindered our students. If we are looking for a direction, we need only ask those who have stepped off the path that the system predetermined for them and set off on their own, beckoning us to follow them. It is easy to hear the messages underlying their stories. They are looking for a world that sees the unique value of every child. They are looking for a world that welcomes all children into the social whirlpool of school experiences. They are looking for a world where justice and equity are not merely ideals but are realities of everyday life. These students do not need the language of academia to convey their lessons. Their simple language instructs us in the simple truth of our purpose as educators. We are called on simply to teach—all students—in the ways that they can learn.

As you travel with our students through the world they have encountered, we invite you to hear the power of their voices and to understand the revolution they encourage in our educational system. These students are standard bearers of humanity in our world, and we are challenged to follow their example in our classrooms and in our daily lives.

REFERENCES

Individuals with Disabilities Education Improvement Act (IDEA) of 2004, PL 108-446, 20 U.S.C. 1400 *et seq.*

Rodis, P., Garrod, A., & Boscardin, M.L. (2001). *Learning disabilities and life stories.* Boston: Allyn & Bacon.

Van Bockern, S.L., Brendtro, L.K., & Brokenleg, M. (2000). Reclaiming our youth. In R.A. Villa & J.S. Thousand (Eds.), *Restructuring for caring and effective education: Piecing the puzzle together* (2nd ed., pp. 56–76). Baltimore: Paul H. Brookes Publishing Co.

Wexler, P. (1992). *Becoming somebody: Toward a social psychology of school.* London: Falmer Press.

I

The Importance
of Student Voices

1

Why Can't They Figure It Out?

Elliott Shelton

I'm a senior in high school. I was first put in special ed. in the third grade. I've been in special ed. for most of my life, and it's been extremely rough for those years. Special ed. really does impact a kid. I will share some stories from my experiences in school. I hope this will help teachers understand how it feels to be labeled "sped."

Because I couldn't read, people would think I couldn't do anything else. I always had a hard time with that. It always made me feel like I should hold back or something. I never was too outgoing or anything like that, especially in middle school because I was always stuck out in the portables. I'm also not a very good speller, so, yeah, I guess I feel I always held back. Like, I never really wanted to tell anyone I could do better or I did have more to offer. Not being able to read and being labeled as a "sped" was always a barrier. I mean, there are a lot of kids, and they look at you different. The teacher looks at you different. That's just how it is. You just have to deal with it. You're just different, and that's it. You can't do the same things in school as everyone else, and it's embarrassing. They like shoot you down. My confidence was shot. You don't want to talk to anybody even if they talk to you. You just look down because you don't know how they're going to react to you. If they're not going to want to talk to you, you're just like "all right." You can't really get mad or anything because you don't want to embarrass them. Like if you tried to talk to someone. I guess I was just always afraid of being let down, so I wouldn't talk.

I've heard teachers say that special education classes boost kids' self-esteem. Special ed. does not boost your self-esteem. It's definitely negative. They say you're supposed to feel at ease with your peers in these classes, but that's not the case. I felt like I was just in with a bunch of kids who couldn't behave themselves. I used to look around and think, "Hey, these aren't my peers; I'm not like this!" The teachers used to like me because I was the only one in there who wasn't a troublemaker. There were a lot of BD (behavior disordered) kids in the class making a ruckus, and I never really got an opportunity to learn. I mean, I wanted to learn. I have dyslexia—not BD—and I was stuck in these classes with these kids who were throwing desks and acting up so they didn't have to do work. I was stuck in these classes with the bad kids who the regular education teachers didn't want disrupting their classes. Unlike me, they actually could read and spell, but the teacher spent so much time trying to keep them under control that I didn't learn anything for years.

I blame that on the schools—the fact that I didn't learn much. I felt like because my reading level was so low, the only material they let me read was really low and babyish. I never got a chance to learn because I was always forced to read these really small words that didn't mean anything. I didn't learn anything except how to read the rinky-dink words. It was so frustrating because I wanted to learn all these cool things that my regular ed. friends were learning, but I was still falling way behind with reading anything more than 4-letter words. I couldn't understand what the words meant, and no one seemed to figure out that I could learn in other ways.

In middle school, it was really pretty rough because I remember when I'd have to go into a regular ed. classroom and two of the other students would take turns reading to me while the other students were reading out of the book, and that was always kind of embarrassing. Special education was never a pleasant experience. I feel like I never got much out of it. Middle school and elementary school seemed like the only point of being in those classes was to make sure the kids didn't get out of line or anything.

I used to be told that things were individualized in special education, but they never were. I used to think that special education teachers were supposed to have more education in teaching, but in my experience that's not the case. It seems like most of them walk right off the street and have no idea how to teach a class.

My sister went to my high school for 2 years, and she was really popular. Before she graduated, she told me, "Make sure you get out of special ed. All those kids in there are dumb; they're dorks, and no one hangs out with them ... you're not going to like it in there, so you've got to get out." I was like, "Oh, thanks! Like I have any choice!!" That was some confidence booster right there. But the thing is, if she tells me that, and she's my sister, then it's pretty obvious that everyone else looks down on the special ed. kids. We don't get involved in school stuff. We don't do homecoming or things like that because nobody knows us.

Teachers can sometimes make things so humiliating for special ed. students. I remember an instance in my junior year when my self-contained class was in the library along with other regular ed. students. My teacher invited someone from the university to evaluate us (or something like that) by having each of us stand up and repeat the ABCs. I remember being SO embarrassed having to do that while being made fun of by the other regular ed. students. I will never forget that experience.

Electives should have been the best part of the day, but it didn't always work out that way. I enjoyed playing the guitar but did not enjoy going to guitar class. I remember the teacher having the class take turns reading from a book that had very hard words describing the history of the guitar. Several other students would try to help me read, which just made me very embarrassed. I knew I couldn't read that material. So instead of enjoying the class, I would dread it sometimes.

I remember signing up for auto mechanics—an elective I thought would be fun and a valuable tool to have in the future. But the teacher was tired of the school throwing in all the kids that were troublemakers into his class, because that's what they did at my school—put all the troublemakers in auto shop. My teacher was upset by that, so he decided to make the first semester all bookwork. I had a really hard time with that because I'm not good with books, and it was overwhelming. So I flunked the class and never had a chance to learn anything about auto mechanics.

My dad was always upset while I was in school. He really wanted me to be in regular ed. and get bad grades versus being in special ed. and not learning anything. He'd rather have me learn. We'd try every year to get me back into regular education at the IEP (individualized education program) meetings. Now, those were always pretty bad. The teachers would all sit around and tell me how low my skills were . . . how I was below grade level on this and that. They would always say my skill levels weren't high enough to be regular ed. and I would be struggling. I know my family and I are supposed to be a part of the IEP committee, but I feel I only had input on my IEPs to a certain extent. The teachers always ruled the meeting. It was always the same thing over and over again. He SHOULD be at grade level at this. He SHOULD be at grade level at that. Then, you end up exactly where you were when you came in. It's like, why did you even have this IEP in the first place? They didn't want to go anywhere or do anything with me.

My parents would be frustrated but always followed the advice of the teachers since they're the experts. Outside of school, they supported me so much. I have gone to plenty of tutors, been diagnosed and rediagnosed several times. My mom even took me to a hearing specialist because she thought I couldn't hear the words right. They tried as hard as they could to bring me up to grade level. But they didn't understand dyslexia and how hard reading is for me. Now, they know and they understand what it's like for me, and things are much better.

In my personal life, I like to do a lot of things. I try to get involved in things outside of school. I am really into grappling. Grappling is submission fighting. It's like wrestling. I like to hang out with my sister, my friends. I like to do a lot of things with them. I have a lot of friends who are out of school. I think we get along so well because we're not in special ed. classes at high school. They know I was in special ed., and they've been cool and supportive. We would make jokes about it—it was nothing to them.

I have learned so much about what makes a good teacher. Good teachers can see your problem and try to work with it. They also can see the good, not just the bad. They get to know you . . . as long as you want them to know you. They try different things.

Some kids can learn but just not the same way. Teachers should give students different ways to learn information. Teachers should do more hands-on, oral, and visual work in classes. For example, I also scuba dive. It's not easy, and you have to take a lot of classes before you become certified. Scuba diving was fun because I actually got a chance to learn. The scuba teacher was such a good instructor.

My dad was friends with the instructor, and they worked something out with me where I could watch the video instead of reading the book and take the test orally instead of reading it myself and failing it. So, I took the test and aced it. I could do all of the physical things just fine, so it all worked out okay. If I could do that in science, social studies, and literature, that would be fine. But teachers seem to see that as cheating. Why can't they figure it out? They think that if you can't read, then you shouldn't be able to take the test.

In school, I do think I could have done things really well, but I feel I haven't been given the chance to succeed because I wasn't given the chance. The teachers didn't give me the opportunity to show what I could do; they just focused on the things I couldn't do. In school, we just read out of books and did worksheets. Tons of worksheets. I hate worksheets. How can a kid who has dyslexia learn anything from worksheet packets? Even though they say they do, my teachers definitely didn't understand dyslexia. I think they had no idea what it is. They think it's this thing where you reverse your *d*s and *b*s. They all need to be educated on what it really is, and how dyslexia is different for different people.

I hope that someday they get rid of special ed. I hate it. It's not a place to put the kids who aren't like everyone else . . . special ed. is just a way of learning. Why do I have to be "special" because I see things differently than someone else? Teachers shouldn't see me as a dyslexic. They need to see me as a person first. Sure, they need to take the dyslexia into consideration, but only to a certain extent. Your personality is who you are.

2

A Parent's View

Katherine Shelton

My son, Elliott Shelton, was diagnosed with learning disabilities in the second grade. We had a feeling this could happen, as his older sister was diagnosed with learning disabilities in the second grade also. She stayed in B-level classes through middle school and was totally in regular ed. in high school.

Elliott had a harder time in school than his sister. He really struggled. We went to meeting after meeting with teachers, tutors, counselors, reading specialists; you name it—we tried it. The school system would not recognize dyslexia as a learning disability, so it was hard to get the help he needed. Finally, he was tested by a former school psychologist who quickly verified he was a classic dyslexic.

He was always a quiet, shy kid in school. I remember when the kindergarten teacher came to meet him at our home before school started—I had to literally drag him out of his room for him to come out and meet her. He was very shy.

Every time I read his chapter or hear him talk about what he went through, it still breaks my heart. I wish I could have waved a magic wand. He was diagnosed with ADD (attention deficit disorder) and took Ritalin and other drugs, but they didn't seem to help. He was not hyperactive, so the drugs made him feel miserable. I thought maybe we had found a cure—but to no avail.

In high school, things started to turn around for Elliott. He was a friendly, well-liked kid who had lots of friends. He was on the wrestling team and learned to play the guitar. At least in high school, the classrooms were integrated on the main campus. He was not placed out in the portables.

Finally, in his senior year, he found a teacher who saw great potential in him. Elliott came to life. He started enjoying going to school and attending class with his favorite teacher, Ms. Moore. We are so grateful to her. She encouraged him to rise above the disabilities. She helped him to realize that he wasn't disabled—he just learned differently. So many others placed so much emphasis on reading and writing.

Ms. Moore took him to a seminar, and the speaker, who couldn't read or spell very well, was a very successful business-man with a degree from Harvard. The speaker said that just because you have trouble reading or writing doesn't mean you can't learn. If he sends an e-mail, it will have spelling errors in it. After hearing the speaker, Elliott felt empowered to share the message to other students and teachers.

He loves to go with Ms. Moore and speak in front of audiences of student teachers or other professionals to tell them what it was like. He encourages the teachers to realize there are different ways of learning. He hopes that he can in some way prevent other students from going through what he did. One of my greatest joys was being in the audience at a teachers' convention in Orlando, Florida, to hear him speak. I hope he will continue on with this enthusiasm.

Thank you for listening.

3

The Human Rights
Basis for Student Personal
Empowerment in Education

Ruth Luckasson

What are human rights? And what do human rights have to do with students and education? Do students with disabilities have human rights? Are there special education implications of human rights?

How we answer these questions about the nature of human rights and who is entitled to human rights is critically important to the approximately 6.5 million students with disabilities receiving special education services in the United States today. The answers are also important to each of us as members of a society, including the friends, teachers, and families of students with disabilities. We each are affected by society's willingness to acknowledge the human rights of students with disabilities and by the ways human rights are expressed or not expressed in schools.

In this chapter, I explore 1) what human rights are and whether there are certain people who are excluded from having human rights, 2) how human rights and education are connected and how typical violations of human rights might look in both the broader world and in schools, 3) the implications of a human rights analysis for special education, 4) what the voices of students teach about human rights, and 5) some recommendations for the future of fairness and justice in schools.

WHAT ARE HUMAN RIGHTS?

A precise list of specific human rights cannot be obtained because different legal philosophers, political leaders, and universal documents use different terms and break down rights into different components. There is general agreement, however, that human rights include various forms of the following: life, liberty, property, and equality (Rawls, 1999). But whatever way they are expressed, and whatever formulation they might take, the concept of human rights refers to the idea that there are some aspects of humanhood and living in a society that are nonnegotiable—certain aspects of being a human being that the social contract must respect.

More than 180 United Nations human rights documents apply to people with disabilities. Some of the documents include the *International Covenant on Civil and Political Rights* (1966a); *International Covenant on Economic, Social and Cultural Rights* (1966b); *Declaration on the Rights of Mentally Retarded Persons* (1971); *Declaration on the Rights of Disabled Persons* (1975); *Convention Against Torture, and Other Cruel, Inhuman, or Degrading Treatment or Punishment* (1984); *International Convention of the Rights of the Child* (1989); *Principles for Protection of Persons with Mental Illness* (1991); *Standard Rules on Equalization of Opportunities for People with Disabilities* (1993); and the *Montreal Declaration on Intellectual Disabilities* (2004) (Herr, Gostin, & Koh, 2003; Quinn, Degener, & Bruce, 2002; United Nations, 2001). American law also contains many protections of human rights: the U.S. Constitution (e.g., 14th Amendment protections of due process and equal protection), federal statutes (e.g., Section 504 of the Rehabilitation Act of 1973 [PL 93-112], the Individuals with Disabilities Education Improvement Act of 2004 [PL 108-446], the Americans with Disabilities Act of 1990 [PL 101-336]), federal regulations, state constitutions, state laws, and state regulations.

In thinking about human rights, we must face some incorrect but probably unconsciously held prejudices. Sometimes people incorrectly place certain conditions on human rights. Consider the following questions: Are human rights only for *certain* people? For example, are only smart people entitled to have human rights? Are human rights only for people of a particular color? Or only for people who have financial assets? Or only for people of a certain age? Do individuals have human rights only if the rights are officially granted by the government in writing? Do individuals have human rights only if they "deserve" them? Or only if they earn them by performing some type of productive work? Do individuals have human rights only if they are "capable" of exercising them? Do they have human rights only if they can object to any denial of human rights? And of particular relevance here, do individuals have human rights only if they do not have a disability that requires special education supports?

The answer to each of these questions is *no*. Human rights apply to all people. In the words of the United Nations' Universal Declaration on Human Rights, Article 1, "All human beings are born free and equal in dignity and rights" (1948). There are no exclusions based on color, intelligence, assets, deservedness, or capability.

CONNECTION BETWEEN HUMAN RIGHTS AND EDUCATION

Education and human rights are intricately intertwined. Education influences human rights, and human rights influence education. Education, in its best sense, is an essential part of preparing individuals to meaningfully exercise their human rights, and their exercise of human rights leads to deeper learning and education.

Education leads to empowerment. Justin Dart, long-time disability activist, stated,

> The business of society is empowerment. The legitimate purpose of human rights, of human society and its governments, is not simply to guarantee equal opportunity to pursue the good life. The purpose, the absolute responsibility of society is to empower all its members actually to produce and to live the good life. (as cited in Oliver, 1996, p. 93)

Goodlad, Mantle-Bromley, and Goodlad argued that the schools a society creates play a critical role in the kind of society that results. They stated,

> The well-being of a *total* culture requires education for all, without exclusivity on the basis of cast: ethnicity, race, sex, heredity, religion, lifestyles and sexual preferences, wealth, assumed intelligence, physical disability, or whatever else humans are able to think up as bases for discrimination. Whatever the medium intended for education, the provision of *total inclusion* is a moral imperative in a democracy and, it is essential to point out, a practical necessity for the health of all and for the continued renewal of a democratic culture. (2004, p. 7; emphasis in original)

Schools teach powerful messages not only through the formal textbook curriculum but also through example. They teach not only students but also students' families, friends, and communities. What do we want our schools to teach about justice, fairness, disability, and democracy? If students with disabilities are labeled and segregated and denied participation in the school's learning, what message is taught about justice?

A beautiful cycle integrally connects education and human rights: Individual learning leads to personal empowerment, which in turn leads to the ability to make meaningful choices, which leads to the ability to take purposeful risks, which leads to more and deeper learning. This cycle is represented in Figure 3.1.

SPECIAL EDUCATION
IMPLICATIONS OF HUMAN RIGHTS

Why is the discussion of human rights important in special education? What is at stake? If one listens to the voices of the students in this book, one could conclude that in the school environment, just like in every other environment in which humans live, everything is potentially at stake. All of the nonnegotiables of being human take a form in school life: life, liberty, property, and equality. The form may be different because of the age of the students, their status in their families, and the supposed "for their own good" nature of education. But consider how the following human rights might

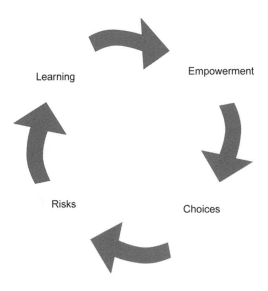

Figure 3.1.   Cycle of education and human rights.

appear in schools and also how violations of these rights might appear:

- Recognition as a human being in the world
- Participation in the human conversation
- Thinking
- Feeling
- Conscience
- Personal autonomy
- Bodily integrity
- Liberty
- Privacy
- Property
- Expression
- Security of one's person
- Association
- Intimacy and marriage
- Health
- Education
- Work
- Social security

Table 3.1 lists frequently mentioned human rights, some examples of typical violations of human rights, and some examples of violations specific to school policies and environments.

STUDENTS SPEAK ABOUT HUMAN RIGHTS

"That's not fair!" Students have well-developed ideas about what is fair. The concept of fairness emerges developmentally at a very young age in humans and is so foundational that it probably has an evolutionary purpose. Fisher (1999) interviewed 257 typically developing high school students in one school in which students with disabilities were educated in general education classes. In his analysis of the data, Fisher found that "human rights" was one of the four

Table 3.1.   Human rights, typical violations, and how violations might look in school policies and environments

Human rights	Typical violations	Possible violations in school policies and environments
Life	Government-imposed death	Denial or delay of lifesaving supports such as ventilator assistance or clean intermittent catheterization
Recognition as a human being in the world	Dehumanization	Sanctioned name-calling and bullying (e.g., *vegetable, retard*), discrimination based on disability, or stigma
Participation in the human conversation	Isolation, exclusion	Isolation rooms, segregated buildings, lack of access to common areas, denial of supports necessary for participation, or denial of augmentative communication systems or supports
Thinking	Political indoctrination	Convincing students to think in a certain way
Feeling	Preventing or denying feelings	Pushing students to feel a certain way or to deny their true feelings
Conscience	Forcing one to take actions against one's beliefs	Forcing students to take actions contrary to their beliefs or imposing a system of segregation on students when they believe it is unfair
Personal autonomy	Preventing personal choices	Preventing student choices, not teaching choice-making skills, or not providing opportunities to safely practice choice making
Bodily integrity	Intruding on a person's body without consent	Doing things to students' bodies without their consent (e.g., imposing toilet assistance without asking permission)
Liberty	Deprivation of freedom	"Programming" a student's days without his or her input, making individualized education program decisions that the student is a not part of, or "sending" a student somewhere else for education
Privacy	Invading a person's thoughts, beliefs, or individual space	Broadcasting students' assessment information, leaving students' toilet doors open, arranging space so that students undress in front of others, or forcing students to make private requests in public
Property	Removing possessions	Removing possessions, adding students' clothes or possessions to the "common pile" without their permission, or randomly taking away students' property as "punishment"
Expression	Prohibiting speech and free ideas	Denying students the means to develop communication and to convey ideas or limiting safe opportunities to express beliefs

Security of one's person	Attacking a person, a family, or a possession	Hitting, yelling at, pushing, or maliciously teasing students; locking students in or out of a room; gossiping about families in school; or destroying student property to "teach everyone a lesson"
Association	Prohibiting meeting with others	Preventing participation in school or extracurricular activities
Intimacy and marriage	Forbidding relationships and the personal closeness that an individual desires	Keeping students separate from each other, creating separate dances or proms based on disability, reporting to disciplinary authorities the handholding of friends with disabilities, or denying sexuality education
Health	Denying health care	Denying school nurse or community health supports, refusing to teach students how to care for their own health, or neglecting education necessary to avoid victimization
Education	Denying learning opportunities	Not teaching academic skills, preventing access to the general curriculum and necessary supports, not providing education needed to exercise citizenship, not preparing students to be adults (e.g., to take their place as adults in society), imposing shorter days on certain students, or "pushing out" certain students so that they drop out
Work	Preventing work contributions	Denying students access to academic and social learning and community connections that lead to employment, giving students meaningless work, making unemployment a condition of receiving care
Social security	Withholding food, shelter, health care, or long-term security from those in need	Withholding food, shelter, health care, or long-term security from students

themes raised by students for why inclusion was a good idea. Generally, the students' reasons focused on the rights of their peers with the disabilities, but one student mentioned something broader, "I have the right to experience human diversity in my school" (p. 462). Students' own use of the language of justice and human rights to explain inclusive education for peers with disabilities is an important statement about their beliefs about fairness and justice for their own school.

In this book, students with disabilities themselves are communicating their conclusions about what is fair or unfair in their schools concerning special education. They are asking that their human rights be acknowledged and respected. What is our response?

TEACHERS SUPPORT HUMAN RIGHTS

Given the interconnectedness of education and human rights, teachers can play a critical role in human rights. I believe that teachers can be important human rights workers. What do human rights workers do? They stand beside other human beings and learn together, teach each other, advocate, communicate, model, participate in the human conversation, and support the participation of others. For students with disabilities, teachers are essential allies in helping them achieve their human rights. Outstanding teachers who support students with and without disabilities see and listen, acknowledge the humanity of each child, assure the physical presence and participation of each child, support the participation of each child in the human conversation by supporting the child's relationships with others, and teach each child the skills for learning, empowerment, choices, and risks, which lead to continued learning. Outstanding teachers also advocate alongside students with disabilities, communicate, model, and—with the students—walk toward justice.

What is justice? According to John Rawls, the principles of justice should be fair. Rawls asserted that in order for there to be *fairness* in society, the principles of justice selected must be considered fair within "the original position," that is, within an imaginary situation in which "no one knows his place in society, his class position or social status, nor does anyone know his fortune in the distribution of natural assets and abilities, his intelligence, strength, and the like" (1971, p. 12). Thus, the principles are fair only when one chooses them without knowing one's own ultimate place and abilities, that is, from "behind a veil of ignorance."

Using this analysis, have we created schools that are fair? Are these schools designed consistent with fairness from "the original position"? Are they consistent with principles that every student would agree are fair even before the student "knows his place in society, his class position or social status, . . . his fortune in the distribution of natural assets and abilities, his intelligence, strength, and the like"? The students who speak in this book say that the actions of many schools are not fair, and they have strong recommendations for how to make schools that are fairer. These students assert principles of justice and human rights.

If justice is ignored in the schools, and if students believe they cannot change the schools for the better, what does that mean for our society in the long term? William Rainey Harper, the first President of the University of Chicago, argued in the context of university–public school partnerships, "Education is the basis of all democratic progress. The problems of education are, therefore, the problems of democracy" (1905, p. 25, as cited in Brabeck, Walsh, & Latta, 2003, p. 96). If our schools cannot organize themselves with justice, can our democratic society hope for adult citizens prepared for justice?

REFERENCES

Americans with Disabilities Act (ADA) of 1990, PL 101-336, 42 U.S.C. §§ 12101 *et seq.*

Brabeck, M.M., Walsh, M.E., & Latta, R.E. (Eds.). (2003). *Meeting at the hyphen: Schools–universities–communities–professions in collaboration for student achievement and well being: 102nd yearbook of the National Society for the Study of Education* (Part II). Chicago: University of Chicago Press.

Fisher, D. (1999). According to their peers: Inclusion as high school students see it. *Mental Retardation, 37,* 458–467.

Goodlad, J.I., Mantle-Bromley, C., & Goodlad, S.J. (2004). *Education for everyone: Agenda for education in a democracy.* San Francisco: Jossey-Bass.

Harper, W.R. (1905). *The trend in higher education.* Chicago: University of Chicago Press.

Herr, S.S., Gostin, L.O., & Koh, H.H. (2003). *The human rights of persons with intellectual disabilities: Different but equal.* New York: Oxford University Press.

Individuals with Disabilities Education Improvement Act of 2004, PL 108-446, 20 U.S.C §§ 1400 *et seq.*

Oliver, M. (1996). *Understanding disability: From theory to practice.* New York: Macmillan.

Quinn, G., Degener, T., & Bruce, A. (2002). *Human rights and disability: The current use and future potential of United Nations human rights instruments in the context of disability.* New York: United Nations.

Rawls, J. (1971). *A theory of justice.* Cambridge, MA: Belknap Press/Harvard University Press.

Rawls, J. (1999). *The law of peoples.* Cambridge, MA: Harvard University Press.

Rehabilitation Act of 1973, PL 93-112, 29 U.S.C. §§ 701 *et seq.*

United Nations. (1948). *Universal declaration of human rights.* Retrieved June 2, 2005, from http://www.un.org/Overview/rights.html

United Nations. (1966a). *International covenant on civil and political rights.* Retrieved June 2, 2005, from http://www.ohchr.org/english/law/ccpr.htm

United Nations. (1966b). *International covenant on economic, social and cultural rights.* Retrieved June 2, 2005, from http://www.ohchr.org/english/law/cescr.htm

United Nations. (1971). *Declaration on the rights of mentally retarded persons.* Retrieved June 2, 2005, from http://www.ohchr.org/english/law/res2856.htm

United Nations. (1975). *Declaration on the rights of disabled persons.* Retrieved June 2, 2005, from http://www.unhchr.ch/tbs/doc.nsf/898586b1dc7b4043c1256a450044f331/aabd321f3203b098c1256ff0004d20b7/$FILE/G0540066.pdf

United Nations. (1984). *Convention against torture, and other cruel, inhuman, or degrading treatment or punishment.* Retrieved June 2, 2005, from http://www.unhchr.ch/tbs/doc.nsf/898586b1dc7b4043c1256a450044f331/aabd321f3203b098c1256ff0004d20b7/$FILE/G0540066.pdf

United Nations. (1989). *International convention of the rights of the child.* Retrieved June 2, 2005, from http://www.ohchr.org/english/law/crc.htm

United Nations. (1991). *Principles for protection of persons with mental illness.* Retrieved June 2, 2005, from http://www.ohchr.org/english/law/principles.htm

United Nations. (1993). *Standard rules on equalization of opportunities for people with disabilities.* Retrieved June 2, 2005, from http://www.ohchr.org/english/law/opportunities.htm

United Nations. (2004). *Montreal declaration on intellectual disabilities.* Retrieved June 2, 2005, from http://www.thearc.org/misc/montreal declaration.pdf

United Nations, General Assembly. (2001, December 19). *Res. 56/168 Ad Hoc Committee appointed to draft proposed "international convention on the protection and promotion of the rights and dignity of persons with disabilities."* New York: Author.

4

Why Educators Need to Incorporate Student Voice into Planning

Reviewing the Literature

Veronica M. Moore

"The problem, after all, is not with the
voices that speak but with the ears that do not hear."
—Casey (1996, p. 223)

Amidst the chaos of curriculum standards and high-stakes testing, I believe it is easy to overlook or underestimate the power of student voices in planning and implementing meaningful classroom instruction. I have found this is especially true when dealing with inclusion. Fortunately, we are beginning to realize the importance of acknowledging students' experiences. In this chapter, I share the critical incident that shaped my view of teaching. In addition, I share a brief review of the prevailing literature about the voices of students with disabilities in educational decision making. Clearly, incorporating student voices in the curriculum can assist in developing a community-based pedagogy and allows teachers to ultimately become more effective in the classroom.

IMPORTANCE OF LISTENING

I learned about the importance of listening to students when I was a high school special education inclusion teacher. One of my high school seniors, Evonne Sanchez, was an integral force that compelled me to reevaluate my own teaching practice and expectations. Evonne was one of the charter members of the "Peer Buddies" group at our high school. In our school district, students with disabilities were typically segregated from their peers for the majority of the day. I was on a mission to bring more inclusion and acceptance of disabilities to the school through a new program that paired "typical" students with peers who had moderate to intensive support needs. The goal of this program was to provide academic assistance, social support, and, ultimately, friendship.

As the Peer Buddies teacher, I studied and prepared relentlessly for the first day of class. I read the literature on peer buddy programs by national experts such as Susan Copeland, Carolyn Hughes, Eric Carter, and Doug Fisher. I attended numerous seminars and conferences to learn all that I could about creating an inclusive, appropriate curriculum that welcomed and acknowledged all of the members of the class. As recommended by the experts, I began the first days of school teaching a disability-awareness curriculum. I went over the nature and needs of students who receive services under the Individuals with Disabilities Education Act Amendments of 1997 (IDEA '97; PL 105-17), spoke with empathy of the injustices historically endured by individuals with disabilities, and created numerous opportunities for the students to develop a sense of understanding of differences and diversity.

Finally, the first day of meeting our "buddies" approached. The students assembled around a big table, and I began the session. While I was carrying out my thoughtful, carefully planned lesson, several of the students with disabilities began acting out. During the 50-minute period, we encountered several outbursts and witnessed significant sensory overload and other behaviors that the untrained eye might have found to be unsettling. When the bell rang and the students filed out of the classroom, I panicked. I was convinced that this program might never work. Although I was a firm believer in inclusion and wanted to help others see the benefits, I was afraid that some of the behaviors from the students with disabilities would alarm the other kids.

After deliberating all night on the most effective strategy to handle this situation, I decided to have a debriefing session about the activities we witnessed. I sat all of the "buddies" down, took a deep breath and began my speech, "There were some things that happened yesterday that were probably hard to handle. I know it may have been difficult for you to be around all of that. Is everyone okay?" I was terrified of the answer I would receive. What if they all wanted to drop the class? What if I were doing it all wrong? The class was silent. Evonne stared at me and shook her head sadly. "Miss," she began slowly, "*You're* the one with the problem. Everything's fine."

I was flabbergasted, but she was absolutely right. I *was* the one with the problem. I was so worried about creating the perfect curriculum that I forgot about the prevailing classroom dynamic that inherently influences the success or failure of a class. I was so worried about ensuring that the class was appropriately fashioned according to my standards of inclusion that I never thought to involve or ask the students in the development process. I forgot the critical element of teaching—that it is not all about *me*—it is about the kids in the classroom.

Evonne went on to explain that the students from the special education class were just a little "freaked out" because they were put with a bunch of strangers. She offered really innovative suggestions on how to make the transition better and even helped me plan curriculum for the remainder of the semester. Evonne made inclusion seem so workable. Moreover, as I continued to listen, her input was invaluable to me for the remainder of the semester.

REEXAMINING PRACTICE: WHAT DOES THE LITERATURE SAY?

Fortunately, most teachers will have an "Evonne" in their classrooms to help them reexamine their teaching practices and the benefits of inclusion. When educators are prepared to let go of their preconceived notions and fears or projections about students with disabilities, the daily routines will run more efficiently. Simply put, to be more effective, teachers need to give more credence to the students' experiences and involve them in educational decision making and curriculum development. Too many students, especially those with disabilities, have limited input into decisions about their placement options when they are in school.

The concept of allowing students to have a say in their own placement or curriculum options energized me in my own teaching practice. Eagerly, I went back to the University of New Mexico's Zimmerman Library and conducted a search on student voice and disabilities. I wanted to read about other studies that showed the importance of the perceptions of students with disabilities regarding their educational placements and experiences. Because I was a strong advocate of inclusive classrooms, I wanted to see if the literature indicated students' preferences of where they would like to receive their special education services.

The method of locating research used in this review followed Klingner's (1999) two-step selection process. Initially, several broad computer searches were done on-line through First Search, using the following descriptors: *adolescents, students, disabilities, high school,* and *perceptions or attitudes.* Abstracts that matched these phrases were reviewed to see if they included students' voices on their perceptions of educational placements. In addition, a hand search of issues from 1999 to 2003 of *Exceptional Children, Journal of Learning Disabilities, Teaching Exceptional Children, Remedial and Special Education,* and *Learning Disability Quarterly,* as well as issues from 2002 to 2004 of *High School Journal* was conducted. This task was accomplished by skimming the table of contents of every available edition of these journals at the University of New Mexico's Zimmerman Library. After examining the abstracts and reference lists of all of the studies that met the appropriate descriptors, the selection of literature was then further refined for this review. The studies chosen to be included in this literature review all demonstrated the importance of the voices of students with disabilities in educational decision making.

Regrettably, the common thread one finds is that labeling kids in the educational system, especially when the label is one of disability, often has serious repercussions on how students view themselves or perceive others as viewing them. The good news, however, is that the summary of literature that follows supports the premise that if teachers would be willing to listen and learn from the students' experiences, school could be a more welcoming institution. It is hoped that teachers can work toward making all students feel as if they are part of the school community.

STUDENT PERCEPTIONS
ARE VALUABLE INFORMATION

Beyond question, the foremost objective of all educators should be to create educational opportunities for children that are inclusive, challenging, and meaningful. What is problematic, however, is that most decisions about an appropriate curriculum seldom include consultation with the students who will be directly affected. The literature in this review consistently demonstrates that students' perceptions contain valuable information that should be used in deciding what works in a classroom. As further evidenced by my experience with Evonne, educators must listen to students' voices and implement what they learn from students' perceptions and experiences to create the best educational services. One should expect that students with disabilities have ideas and opinions concerning their own education. What is surprising is that their voices are too often omitted from the literature.

Albeit limited, research repeatedly indicates that students with disabilities do have distinct ideas and opinions concerning their educational experience. Coinciding with the spirit of the IDEA '97, students should have an active voice in the appropriate placement and services necessary to achieve academic challenges. Even though myriad approaches to successful curriculum development for students with disabilities exist, there is little evidence that those approaches include student opinions or evaluations. According to Tomlinson (1982), the lack of information on the perspectives of children with disabilities on their school experiences is extremely upsetting, especially at a time of crucial reform in traditional special education. In fact, the perceptions of students with disabilities about school is a new phenomenon in special education research.

Studies have demonstrated that students have very distinct ideas about the ways they should receive their education. Klingner (1999) conducted a synthesis of 20 studies that investigated the perceptions of students from kindergarten to twelfth grade toward instructional methods in general education classes. The research indicated that modifications and special materials were not perceived as being harmful or stigmatizing to the students interviewed. Moreover, students expressed a distinct preference for the environments and methods with which they learned best. Although Klingner cautioned that student preferences should not be the sole indicator for how teachers make all educational and curricular decisions, he advised that students' voices should be considered in decision-making and placement procedures.

CREATING PARTNERSHIPS

As mentioned previously, IDEA '97 is supposed to provide students with more input regarding their educational placements. Unfortunately, as evidenced by the chapters written by Elliott (Chapter 1) and Gary (Chapter 6), this outcome does not always happen. One important way that students can have more voice in educational decision making is through the student-led individualized education program (IEP) process. Hapner and Imel (2002) implemented the student-led IEP process in their high school. Eight students participated in the process, then wrote in journals and spoke about their experiences. When the students realized that they could play an important role in the educational decision-making process, they changed the way they viewed school. The students became less disenfranchised with the educational system and perceived a new-found respect from their teachers. The researchers determined that allowing students to voice their concerns and to have choices of placement caused a new level of partnership to develop between the students and the educational staff.

Lefrello and Miles (2003) also found that partnerships between students and teachers can have a major effect on the transition from middle to high school. The researchers interviewed 12 eighth graders. Half of the respondents had learning disabilities. Regardless of whether they received special education services, the participants provided very similar responses to the interview questions. Both groups expressed trepidation about attending high school. They were concerned about social relationships and opportunities to be involved in school-based activities. The researchers concluded that middle school teachers must collaborate with their students and high school staff to create activities that prepare the eighth graders for the transition. The teachers must provide opportunities to facilitate discussions that address the students' concerns about social interactions, extracurricular activities, and curriculum changes. These discussions will only be effective if they are related to the students' needs. Therefore, an open dialogue among all of the participants in the transition process is essential.

Creating partnerships between students and teachers is crucial for good teaching practice. When these partnerships are expanded to the university setting, preservice teachers can hear powerful insights that can help shape their potential teaching practice (Keefe, Moore, Duff, & Pitcher, 2004). Cook-Sather (2003) agreed with this sentiment. She reported the results of a 7-year study in which students participated in a project titled "Teaching and Learning Together." This project allowed students from diverse backgrounds to assume the roles of teacher educators for preservice teachers. They addressed such topics as learning differences, inclusion, and advanced placement classes. Although the students offered very diverse views regarding these issues, Cook-Sather (2003) stressed that allowing these students to express their feelings toward school and the willingness of preservice teachers to consider these perspectives were the key elements of the project. She emphasized that educators must find avenues to incorporate students' perspectives in more educational policies and practices.

Often, the voices of students with disabilities are not solicited when creating appropriate special education services. Unfortunately, the negative connotation of the word *disability* is still preserved at the school setting and often perpetuates preconceived notions of what students can or cannot achieve. Gerber and Reiff's (1991) ethnography on three individuals with learning disabilities revealed that although the respondents had different adult experiences, they shared similarities in the frustration and lack of empathy demonstrated by the traditional school system. The participants suffered both as students and as adults because they learned differently from the traditional way most individuals learn. The conclusion was that learning disabilities did not prevent learning from taking place, but the educational system played a major role in making learning difficult. Gerber and Reiff (1991) also stressed the importance of listening to the stories and voices of those who have lived the experience rather than trying to substitute one's own analysis.

TEACHERS' INFLUENCE

Accepting a disability can be difficult enough, but it can be further exacerbated if educators do not show empathy or understanding in school. Higgins, Raskind, and Goldberg (2002) gathered data from a 20-year longitudinal study of students with learning disabilities to describe and shed light on the "life-span experiences" of students to use for future policy decisions for all individuals with learning disabilities. Their main goal was to find out how people learned to accept their disabilities. The results indicated that there was a direct correlation with the participants' levels of success and their acceptance and understanding of their disabilities. Unfortunately, the researchers' conclusions also revealed that individuals with learning disabilities have difficulties dealing with stigma and negative attitudes directed toward them because of their label. Based on interviews and conversations with the participants, the researchers stressed that general educators and regular classroom teachers must realize how their actions affect their students even into adulthood.

Rodis, Garrod, and Boscardin (2001) approached the same issue from a phenomenological perspective. They gathered the stories of 13 individuals with learning disabilities to determine how being labeled with a disability affected their education and their life beyond high school. This 3-year study originated from a desire to dissipate common misconceptions about learning disabilities. The stories compiled by the respondents illustrated that the labeling process had significant effects on the participants. For some, the label was stigmatizing and caused shame and anger. For others, however, the label brought relief and legitimacy to why they were struggling in school. Although all of the narratives presented important implications for teachers, only two respondents specifically reflected on their experiences in general education. Both participants indicated that they felt "normal" in general education. Although one of the participants indicated he was angry that he did not receive adequate accommodations, he stressed that his overall experiences in general education were positive.

Kortering and Braziel (1999) examined the factors that could make school a more welcoming environment and reduce the dropout rate. They interviewed 52 ninth graders who received special education services to gain a glimpse into the best and worst part of schools. The participants, who attended a school with a high dropout rate, offered insight about what they needed to enjoy their educational experiences. Not surprisingly, the common theme of the interviews was that the main draw to school was the opportunity to socialize with peers. The participants did indicate, however, that they wished they had teachers who had better attitudes and would be more helpful to the students in the classroom. If more teachers focused on the students' perceptions of their classes, created a curriculum that grabbed the students' attention, and were willing to answer questions, it is possible that the students would be more willing to finish high school.

Kortering and Braziel (2002) said that student insight is paramount when it comes to educational decision making. They spoke to 185 high school students with disabilities about their school experiences to gain insight into their perceptions of their educational programs. The students indicated that they wanted to be in classes where they could be active and experience success. Although socialization rather than learning was found to be the best part of school, the respondents indicated that they liked classes that let them experience success and teachers who were caring and explained things. Overwhelmingly, teachers who were viewed as mean, uncaring, or difficult were the "worst part of school." When asked what could be different, a major theme was change in teacher attitude and classes.

Although it was true there were some limitations to the study, as the youth represented only two high schools, the findings present some significant implications for practice. Most of the participants wanted to succeed in high school. By listening to the voices of their students, educators are in a better position to empower students to take a more active role in decision making, thus ensuring them a better chance of success in the classroom.

There are many classroom set-ups for students. One that is gaining momentum across the country is team teaching. Most of the prevailing literature in this area describes what team teaching looks like from an educator's point of view (e.g., Gately & Gately, 2001; Keefe & Moore, 2004; Mastropieri & Scruggs, 2001). To gain a different perspective on collaborative teaching models, Gerber and Popp (1999) investigated students and their parents' perceptions on the efficacy of these models. They interviewed 123 students in kindergarten through twelfth grade and their parents in focus groups. All of the participants indicated in their interviews that they preferred collaborative teaching. Furthermore, the students with and without disabilities felt that they were doing better academically and wanted the model to continue into the next year. Although the students said the biggest frustration was that they were not allowed to get away with things, such as throwing paper airplanes in class, overall, they were pleased with this type of setting. These authors also suggested that future researchers should take all students' opinions into consideration when designing teaching models.

EFFECT OF
EDUCATIONAL SETTINGS AND SERVICES

Much controversy exists about the appropriate learning environment for students with disabilities. Although some literature supports self-contained settings for academic and social skills (e.g., Baker & Zigmond, 1995; Crocket & Kauffman, 1999; Hallahan, 1998), many students with disabilities prefer being in classrooms with their "typical" peers. In an effort to determine perceptions of high school students in an inclusive versus self-contained setting, Shoho, Katims, and Wilks (1997) sampled 76 high school students with learning disabilities at a rural high school in south central Texas. The students were administered the Dean Alienation Scale (Dean, 1961) to determine their perceptions of isolation, normlessness, and powerlessness. The students who were placed in a resource room, rather than an inclusive setting, indicated more negative perceptions toward school.

Perhaps, if the participants were given more choices in the types of settings, their responses may have been different. For instance, the students were not given a positive alternative when asked how they felt in class. Moreover, when reviewing the mean scores, there was not a major discrepancy between students who claimed they experienced total alienation in either setting. It would seem that if the students felt they had some control over the quality of their education, the study would have revealed the respondents having a more optimistic attitude toward school.

Howard and Tryon (2002) examined the correlation between depressive symptoms and type of classroom placement for students with learning disabilities. The students in this study were asked to self-report the severity of depressive symptoms they experienced. Questionnaires were administered to the students and their counselors. Upon examination of the data, the researchers found that there were no significant differences in depression scores of students in a self-contained setting or in an inclusive classroom.

Of course, negative experiences with special education programs are not limited to students with learning disabilities. Marks, Shrader, Longaker, and Levine (2000) conducted a case study regarding the perceptions of students with Asperger syndrome toward the services they received in school. The researchers created portraits of the three respondents in order to provide a window into their school experiences. Sadly, all of the participants characterized their school experiences as being lonely and isolated. The researchers concluded that the classroom teachers have a profound effect on the classroom climate. They also stressed the importance of listening to personal stories and how they can be extremely influential in helping all educators provide appropriate services to students with disabilities.

Having autonomy and control is important for any individual. Ruef and Turnbull (2002) focused on the experiences and voices of nine individuals with cognitive disabilities and/or autism to determine appropriate and meaningful supports. By listening to the participants' personal narratives, the researchers were allowed an intimate glimpse at how these students with disabilities actually felt about what supports were beneficial and possible solutions for an improved quality of life. The participants indicated that the services they received were not really individualized. Basic needs were being met, but the individuals were not given control over the type of support they received. The participants indicated that the people or agencies implementing the services seemed more concerned with compliance rather than meeting actual needs. They were passionate while discussing their lives and welcomed the chance to offer their suggestions as to how things could be improved.

As a result, the researchers concluded that it is crucial for individuals with disabilities to be given a voice when determining intervention approaches. They further concluded, using this research as an indicator, that individuals with disabilities do not want to be passive recipients of special education services. Instead, it is important that individuals with disabilities are given choices and are active participants in the decision-making process.

FOSTERING ACCEPTANCE

In reality, there will always be a certain percentage of students who are less accepting of diversity. If the teacher hears comments that indicate discord among classmates, these comments should not indicate that inclusion is impossible. Rather, teachers should view the situation as an opportunity to listen to and use classmates' remarks to create increased opportunities for acceptance. Some students initially avoid general education classes because they fear they will not be accepted by the teachers or peers (Moore & Keefe, 2004). Klingner, Vaughn, Schumm, Cohen, and Forgan (1998) investigated the preferences of students with learning disabilities toward inclusion and self-contained settings. When the students were interviewed, the majority of older respondents indicated that the resource room was more positive and preferable over the general education classroom. A group of students with learning disabilities who were first totally included, then assigned to the resource room, unanimously declared that the resource room alleviated frustration and made it easier to make friends.

Moore and Keefe (2004) also found similar results. When they interviewed high school seniors in a self-contained language arts classroom, the students indicated that they felt the resource room teachers were more understanding and patient. Interestingly, the seniors did not prefer the resource room because it provided them increased academic skills; they liked the special education classrooms because of the teachers' willingness to provide modifications and teach to learning styles. The majority of the respondents claimed they wished they could be in general education classes but felt that the teachers would not be as accommodating.

Notably, many proponents of inclusion claim that it fosters acceptance of diversity and the social acceptance of all children (e.g., Fisher, 1999; Lipsky & Gartner, 1995; Villa & Thousand, 1995, 2000).

Nevertheless, when Klingner et al. (1998) interviewed a girl who was a sixth grader in an inclusive classroom, the girl referred to the students without disabilities as *us* and the students with learning disabilities as *them*. Social acceptance is supposed to be the driving force for inclusion. This girl's comment shows some insight about the actual acceptance of students who have traditionally been segregated in the general classroom. The information offered by this girl should not be seen as an excuse for the continued segregation of students. Rather, this insight could be helpful in assisting a teacher in creating a more welcoming classroom where the students are not stigmatized for being different and there is no delineation between "us" and "them."

SUMMARY AND RECOMMENDATIONS

Potentially, the perceptions of students with disabilities about school have a great deal to contribute to the teaching field. This is an emerging area of research in education. At present, a limited number of research studies regarding the voices of students with disabilities exist. This paucity of information, however, does not indicate the lack of importance. Students' perceptions and experiences, both positive and negative, can be helpful in planning challenging curricula and afford students the opportunity to truly become part of the school community. By gaining a greater understanding of the experience of living with a disability, educators can gain sharper insights into how to provide appropriate services.

A true sense of collaboration between students and teachers leads to a deeper understanding of students' daily realities. When teachers solicit the students' opinions and incorporate their voices into educational decision making, students feel more empowered and become less disenfranchised from the educational system. Effective teaching involves communication among colleagues. Students, however, must not be left out of the decision-making process. Evonne taught me the value of collaboration at a whole new level. As her reaction indicated, students sometimes see situations in the classroom in an entirely different way than the teacher. As a result, teachers must take a more vested interest in the voices of students regarding their role in educational decision making.

REFERENCES

Baker, J.M., & Zigmond, N. (1995). The meaning and practice of inclusion for students with learning disabilities: Themes and implications from the five cases. *Journal of Special Education, 29*(2), 163–180.

Casey, K. (1996). The new narrative research in education. *Review of Research in Education, 21,* 211–253.

Cook-Sather, A. (2003). Listening to students about learning differences. *Teaching Exceptional Children, 35*(4), 22–26.

Crockett, J.B., & Kauffman, J.M. (1999). *The least restrictive environment.* Mawhah, NJ: Lawrence Erlbaum Associates.

Dean, D.G. (1961). Alienation: Its meaning and measurement. *American Sociological Review, 26,* 753–777.

Fisher, D. (1999). According to their peers: Inclusion as high school students see it. *Mental Retardation, 37*(6), 458–467.

Gately, S.E., & Gately, F.J. (2001). Understanding co-teaching components. *Teaching Exceptional Children, 33,* 40–47.

Gerber, P.J., & Popp, P.A. (1999). Consumer perspectives on the collaborative teaching model: Views of students with and without LD and their parents. *Remedial and Special Education, 20*(5), 288–296.

Gerber, P.J., & Reiff, H.B. (1991). *Speaking for themselves: Ethnographic interviews with adults with learning disabilities.* Ann Arbor: University of Michigan Press.

Hallahan, D.P. (1998). Sound bytes from special education reform rhetoric. *Remedial and Special Education, 19*(2), 67–69.

Hapner, A., & Imel, B. (2002). The students' voices: "Teachers started to listen and show respect." *Remedial and Special Education, 23*(2), 122–126.

Higgins, E.L., Raskind, M.H., & Goldberg, R.J. (2002). Stages of acceptance of a learning disability: The impact of labeling. *Learning Disability Quarterly, 25*(1), 3–18.

Howard, K.A., & Tryon, G.S. (2002). Depressive symptoms in type of classroom placement for adolescents with learning disabilities. *Journal of Learning Disabilities, 35*(2), 185–190.

Individuals with Disabilities Education Act Amendments of 1997, PL 105-17, 20 U.S.C. §§ 1400 *et seq.*

Keefe, E.B., & Moore, V. (2004). The challenge of co-teaching in inclusive classrooms at the high school level: What the teachers told us. *American Secondary Education, 32*(3), 77–88.

Keefe, E.B., Moore, V., Duff, F.R., & Pitcher, E. (November, 2004). *Using experiential education to enhance teacher preparation for general and special educators.* Paper presented at the Teacher Education Division of the Council for Exceptional Children annual conference, Albuquerque, NM.

Klingner, J.K. (1999). Students' perceptions of instruction in inclusion classrooms: Implications for students with learning disabilities. *Exceptional Children, 66*(1), 23–37.

Klingner, J.K., Vaughn, S., Schumm, J.S., Cohen, P., & Forgan, J.W. (1998). Inclusion or pull out: Which do students prefer? *Journal of Learning Disabilities, 31,* 148–158.

Kortering, L.J., & Braziel, P.M. (1999). Staying in school: The perspective of ninth grade students. *Remedial and Special Education, 20*(2), 106–113.

Kortering, L.J., & Braziel, P.M. (2002). A look at high school programs as perceived by youth with learning disabilities. *Learning Disability Quarterly, 25*(3), 177–188.

Lefrello, T.M., & Miles, D. (2003). The transition from middle school to high school: Students with and without disabilities share their perceptions. *The Clearing House, 76*(4), 212–218.

Lipsky, D.K., & Gartner, A. (1995). Common questions about inclusion: What does the research say? *Exceptional Parent, 61*(1), 36–39.

Marks, S.U., Shrader, C., Longaker, T., & Levine, M. (2000). Portraits of three adolescent students with Asperger's syndrome: Personal stories and how they can inform practice. *JASH, 25*(1), 3–17.

Mastropieri, M.A., & Scruggs, I.E. (2001). Promoting inclusion in secondary classrooms. *Learning Disability Quarterly, 24*, 265–274.

Moore, V., & Keefe, E.B. (2004). "Don't get your briefs in a bunch": What high school student with disabilities have to say about where they receive their services. *Issues in Secondary Education, 13*(1), 7–18.

Rodis, P., Garrod, A., & Boscardin, M.L. (2001). *Learning disabilities and life stories.* Boston: Allyn & Bacon.

Ruef, M.B., & Turnbull, A.P. (2002). The perspectives of individuals with cognitive disabilities and/or autism on their lives and their problem behavior. *Research and Practice for Persons with Severe Disabilities, 27*(2), 125–140.

Shoho, A.R., Katims, D.S., & Wilks, D. (1997). Perceptions of alienation among students with learning disabilities in inclusive and resource settings. *High School Journal, 81*(1), 28–36.

Tomlinson, S. (1982). *A sociology of special education.* Boston: Routledge & Kegan Paul.

Villa, R.A., & Thousand, J.S. (1995). The rationales for creating inclusive schools. In J.S. Thousand & R.A. Villa (Eds.), *Creating an inclusive school* (pp. 28–44). Alexandria, VA: Association for Supervision and Curriculum Development.

Villa, R.A., & Thousand, J.S. (2000). Setting the context: History of and rationales for inclusive schooling. In R.A. Villa & J.S. Thousand (Eds.), *Restructuring for caring and effective education: Piecing the puzzle together* (2nd ed., pp. 7–37). Baltimore: Paul H. Brookes Publishing Co.

5

Stop Asking Me If I Need Help

Angela Gabel

When you see me, I think the first thing you would notice is that I'm a pretty positive person. I love to listen to music, go horseback riding, and draw. In fact, art has been my passion for as long as I can remember. When I hear some of the stories from my friends who have been in special education, I think I've been pretty lucky throughout school. Even though I use a wheelchair, I never was separated from anyone else. I was put in a special ed. preschool for a little while, but it wasn't for me, and my mom got me out of there. When I was in elementary school, my experiences were all right. I had friends and liked to play the same games as everyone else, but the teachers were always worried that I was too fragile and would hurt myself.

I used to love to swing, but I did it a different way. Instead of sitting on the swing, I would lie on it on my stomach. I still could go really high, and it was so much fun. The teachers kind of freaked out when they saw me and told my mother that if I wanted to swing any more I would have to wear a helmet to protect myself. My mother asked the teachers if any of the other kids had to wear helmets. Have you ever seen any little preschooler wearing one of those while swinging? Of course not! My mother said if the other kids didn't have to wear them, then neither did I. I think that was the very beginning of my mission to prove that I'm just like everyone else.

Since it looks like I need a lot of assistance to be self-sufficient, adults at the schools were always hovering around trying to do everything for me. Even as far back as kindergarten, I had a one-on-one aide who would never leave my side. I remember that it would drive me crazy, but since I was so young, I didn't do much to stop her.

Once I got to second grade, I finally became more independent. That year was the changing experience in my life. It's easy for kids to let others do things for them and fall into the "I can't do it" attitude. Except once in a while you get a teacher who won't fall for it. Mr. H. didn't fall for it. He pushed me to try things that were outside of my comfort zone, and, even though I cried and complained, he didn't let me quit.

One of the most important things he taught me was either I did something or I didn't. He wouldn't fall for any of that "I tried" crap. One day, I was getting really frustrated and complained that the work was just too hard. He stared at me for a couple of minutes and set a pencil on his desk. "Try to pick it up," he told me. Well, I leaned over and picked it up. There was never "I tried"—he told me either you did it or you didn't. That has been an important lesson I will never forget.

Since I don't use my arms, I use my mouth to do just about everything. Mr. H. taught me to use my mouth to actually write my own notes, open and close my backpack, and just about anything else other people use their hands to do. Little by little, I became more independent. I learned how to type with my nose, began to draw, and got into all the assistive tech that helped me become really proficient on a computer. Slowly, my confidence blossomed, and I was doing more and more things on my own.

Then, the unthinkable happened. Seventh grade started, and my teacher took one look at me and assumed I required all this assistance. I kept on telling her that I didn't need help with things. I was perfectly competent at opening my own binder, writing notes, or turning the pages of the textbooks. I don't know why people can't get it through their heads that I'm not totally helpless. She was pretty amazed when she could see what I could achieve. Still, I'm not sure if she ever realized all that I was capable of doing.

Once I started high school, things still weren't going very well. Again, I couldn't understand why the adults at the school thought I couldn't do anything for myself. I had lots of friends, and they seemed to get it, but the teachers or the aides always took a long time to catch on. I tried politely talking to the educational assistant assigned to me. I was really direct and told her, "I don't need that much help, but when I do, I'll ask for it." Still, that wasn't good enough. She assumed she knew best and would be there "just in case." Can you imagine how frustrating that is? To have someone hovering around you in the event that something just "might" happen?

It got to the point where I couldn't take it anymore. I felt like I was going to explode, so I burst into the special education office. I screamed at the special education lady in charge and told her how things were going. I hated to be mean, but I had to let her know how I felt about this aide being with me every second of the day. After a lengthy tirade, she called my mom. The three of us decided that I didn't need someone with me all the time and that I would have a peer buddy to help me with the day-to-day activities that go on in the classroom. This was such a relief. Finally, my educational aide shadow was lifted.

We moved to New Mexico last year. It's scary being uprooted from all of your friends and family, but it was a new adventure, and I was actually looking forward to it. I went to my new school and had our first IEP (individualized education program) meeting with the special education department chairperson. At the beginning of the meeting, it was suggested that I have a full-time educational assistant to help me get through the day, and that's how my year began.

Once again, I had to fight to prove I could do things for myself. The people at the school thought I needed help with just about everything—even help getting from class to class and getting my stuff out of my backpack. Once again I was assigned a full-time aide. It was hard enough going to a new school, but try and make friends with an aide following you around from class to class and sitting next to you every day. I couldn't stand it. I would try to have private conversations with my friends, and the aide would always listen in. I'm too old for a babysitter. I needed some privacy at school. I felt like I had traveled back in time and was devastated. My mom and I had to fight the same old battle once again. Since we went through it before, at least this time it was easier. I got my independence and got to make lots of new friends without the aide.

I have to admit that special education does have some good qualities, but it also has a lot of not-so-good qualities. If it wasn't for special education, students with disabilities would never get the chance to get an education. Unfortunately, some of the students who are in special education classes are in there for really dumb reasons, like if a student can't read and he's in there instead of learning how to read in a regular class. Just because you can't read, it doesn't mean you have to be stuck somewhere away from everyone else in school. In fact, just because you're different, you shouldn't be put in a separate classroom far away from kids without disabilities.

It's funny how the teachers just assume that they know what's best for kids because they're the experts. If the teachers would actually sit down with the student and talk for a little while, they would figure out where the problem is and the best way to fix it. Educational aides need to stop babying the students. If you think that they are capable of doing something on their own, then encourage them to do it. Don't ever discourage a student from wanting to try things—even if that means the student may fail at first. If it looks like they need help or if they're not sure how to do a certain step in the process, help them, but don't do it for them.

My family has always been so supportive of me, and I think that has a lot to do with my independence. My parents have pushed and encouraged me to be the best that I can. When I was starting school, my mom wanted me to do as much as I could possibly do on my own. My parents, to this day, still do that. They don't treat me any differently from my three younger siblings, and I wouldn't want them to. I mean, they do some things that I'm not able to participate in, but that's okay. I know my limitations, but I know what I am good at, too. I do like to try new things. It's the only way to know if I can do a certain thing, and I have to try to find out. How do you ever know if you can or can't do something if you never give it a chance?

The most important advice I would give to parents of kids with disabilities is to help their children grow in any way that they can. Always expose them to new things, and let the teachers at the schools know their strengths and what they can do instead of always talking about what they can't do. Nobody really knows a child the same way as a parent.

6

Live to Ride

Gary Hartzog

I'm a senior in high school, and I'm writing this chapter about being in special education. Well, special education has been a huge thing in school, but school isn't my life. There's a lot more to me than what goes on in school. It's just funny how I can be really good at doing things outside of school, but in school I'm considered "special."

In the year 1984, on a hot August day, I was born in Albuquerque, New Mexico. Of course, I don't remember anything about that day, but my parents tell me it was one of the best days they ever had. My earliest memories come at around age 2. I remember that I could ride a bicycle—not a tricycle, mind you. I didn't even need training wheels. I've rarely been off a bike since that day. I even rode my bike into a pool when I was 3 or 4. It wasn't any fun. It was winter, and I tried to ride across the cover, but I fell in. Even though it was freezing, it didn't stop me from riding.

As you can probably guess, I love to ride bikes. In fact, my life is motocross. Motocross is racing with dirt bikes and competing with other riders. I've been riding for about 8 years and compete nationally and locally. My parents never miss a race. The three of us, day in and day out. My dad is my coach, my driver, and my mechanic. My mom's the manager, the cleaning lady, or anything else we need. They're pretty proud of me. Our motto is "The seventh day is for racing." It's like our religion.

Riding is what means the most to me. It's what I love and what I do best, and school just interrupts my real life. School has always been pretty tough. You got six periods—too much work, and I couldn't do it. The work was always hard for me. I can't read very well, so it's always been hard. I was in regular education for math, but that's a different story. My brain just clicks to math, but it's never really clicked to reading. My most vivid memory of school was when a kid in my second grade class stabbed me in the back with scissors. It wasn't life threatening, thanks to the rounded tips of the little kid's scissors, but it was horrible nonetheless.

It was that same year that I got moved out of regular education to special education. Now, that wasn't fun. I don't remember that much about back then, but I do remember the test. They took me to this big school and kept giving me this test over and over. Even though it was years ago and I can't remember a lot of things, those tests are one of those things you just can't get rid of. Those tests. Over and over. I was mad and afraid at the same time. I just wanted to get out of there, and I felt so weird. I was the only person in the room.

One day, I was in regular education, and I was with all my normal friends. Then, I took that test, and the next day I went to this other class. It was smaller. My parents were told that I had a learning disability and ADD (attention deficit disorder) or something like that. All of the kids in my new class were in wheelchairs and stuff like that. I've always been a friendly kid and get along with everybody, so I didn't have any problem getting along with all of the new people in there. The only thing is that I lost all of my old friends. I didn't hang around with my normal friends anymore. Now I had special ed. friends.

Not everything was totally bad, though. I had a good teacher, Miss R. Miss R. had a swan in her backyard, and I thought that was the most wonderful thing I ever heard about . . . other than bicycles. Then, they held me back in fifth grade. They said I wasn't mature enough. What does that mean, "not mature enough"? I would never hold a kid back. I'm sorry, I just won't. My kids are not going to be held back. If I had a chance to do things over again, I would definitely redo fifth grade. All the other kids got to make a mortarboard for fifth-grade graduation ceremony

except for me. It was the worst day of my life. I did get to make one the next year, but it wasn't the same. It would have meant so much more if I got to do it with my "real" fifth-grade class. Because of that, everything changed. I don't know how it would have gone if I got to move up with my friends, but I do know that my life would be totally different right now.

Finally, I made it to middle school. Bike riding still meant the world to me, and my teacher, Miss Smith, really helped me out. She was a cool teacher and down to earth. She always related stuff to my perspective. I had just begun to ride competitively, and she was good at helping me see how my schoolwork related to riding. All of my cool teachers can relate their stuff to bike riding. Because that's all I think ... ride, ride, ride. She'd get math in me that way. She'd give an example like "you have three trophies and five races" and I'm like, "Oh, I get it ... why didn't you say that in the first place?" She was good because she knew how to make it interesting, and she got me learning.

At the end of eighth grade, I began going to my IEP meetings. Up until this year, I didn't even know what an IEP was. My teacher told me it's an individual education program. I don't think it is individual. It's like all teachers talking about YOU, and you can't say anything. My parents would always go to the IEPs. This last time my mom was on my side, but she's always been on the teachers' side. She's always supported me, but the teachers are the professionals, so she thought what they said was right. My mom and dad have always supported me. The funny thing is even at all my IEP meetings, they never moved me even though the teachers always said I was doing good.

So school was okay. I showed up every day and did what the teacher told me to do, but riding was my life. By the time I made it to high school I was dominating my class in racing and got my first broken bone—my leg. I hobbled around on crutches for 6 weeks, but I had fast ones that I filled with racing stickers. By my sophomore year, I matured a lot more. I got my first Yamaha 125cc bike. It was great fun, but I managed to break another bone and spend more time on crutches. I also had my first broken helmet and nose.

School was finally starting to get better, and I found out I had a real talent for math. I began racing nationally and winning more events locally. I finally made it back into regular ed. for algebra. I didn't think I could do it, but before the second semester started I was bumped up to an ever higher math class. In fact, I did well and passed it with no problem!! I was consistently winning at racing and got an official sponsorship with a Suzuki dealership in Colorado. I had a great summer and won two championships in Tularosa, New Mexico. I thought I was invincible.

Well, I wasn't invincible. At the beginning of my senior year, I had a serious accident on my pedal bike. I wasn't even racing! I was riding a regular pedal bike without a helmet and thought I could be better than my friend in jumping over a curb gap, but I ended up on my head and in a coma. Actually, I don't remember what happened, but my friend told me I hit the curb and went up about 10 feet in the air and landed straight on my head. I was in the hospital for a week and then had 9 weeks of homebound school and my mother's constant care. They told me I cracked my skull in three sections, had a concussion, broke my nose, compressed my sixth disk, chipped my teeth, chipped a piece of my first vertebrae, and I would have permanent brain damage. My eyes were swollen shut, and they thought I would be blind. There was just so much. I had to learn how to hold my head up again and how to focus my eyes. I had horrendous headaches for weeks straight.

The first thing I told my parents in the hospital was "SELL MY BIKES." I got better every day, though, and I was told I could never ride again, never be able to drive a car or do a lot of the things I really liked. That answer wasn't good enough to me. Even though I was told I was never riding a bike again, I just couldn't live with that answer. Then, one day when I still had my neck brace on, I went outside and asked my dad if I could ride my bike. I wanted to see if I had fear or not. Well, I had fear.

For the longest time, I just rode down the street. Came back. Parked it. I did that for a while. Then, I asked my mom if she could let me go just one time further down the street. I rode the bike down the street, dropped it down, and cocked my head back. She just stood there shaking her finger at me and said, "Get in the garage. You're not riding for a week." But she was okay. She always encouraged me to do my best no matter what happened to me. Even though she was scared, she supported me once again.

I went back to school and back into my special education classes. The weird thing is that since the accident, things have gotten easier for me in school. I don't know if it's because I got hit on the head or if it's because I changed my outlook toward life. Sometimes you just don't realize how bad things could be until something really scary happens to you. I still have a hard time remembering things. I have to get directions written down or I'll forget what I'm doing. But I'm not afraid. Things are getting better slowly, and I know that I have to keep on trying to do things I used to be able to do or else I'll never get stronger. Soon, I won't have to worry about school, and all I can think about is my real life getting ready to start.

7

If You Want the Fire, Just Reach Deep in Your Heart

Carson Proo

I was born in Albuquerque, New Mexico, on December 10, 1985. When I was born, my mom and dad were a little scared because they knew I had Down syndrome. In my chapter, I will tell you about my life and all the things I do. I have learned and done a lot in my life.

When I was small, I went to school at Peppermint Stick, and I got lost in the playground. My old teachers, they helped me out like being smart and being cool. When I was little, I learned to say a few words like *cup, hats, dogs, future,* things that I can talk about. The other things that I learned were how to swim and how to cook. I learned to be clean, tie my shoes, and dress nice. The other thing I learned was to climb things like climbing on walls at the Stone Age Climbing Center.

I surprise people with what I can do. When I was 10 and at K-Mart with my mom and waiting for her to come back, I went to the cashier and wrote out my mom's check, and the cashier took it! Now, I have my own checks and my new debit card, and I use it sometimes but try not to use it too much.

I have reading skills and writing skills. I write poems and stories about my life and different kinds of things. I like writing about the mind and body. Here is my Poem of the Spirit:

When the spirit leaves
Then the heart stays.
But we will focus on the strong mind
Then you will become one of me.
I meditate on the emptiness of the mind
And I focus on the fire in my mind.
And when the fire gets hot
Then I will be relaxed.

I have done a lot in my 18 years and will tell you about my life and share more poems.

My spiritual life is about karate. I started karate when I was about 10 years old. Now, I do karate at Shotokan Karate in New Mexico. I have a karate master named Funakoshi. Nine years I have been practicing karate. On June 18, 2003, I earned my black belt, and I feel proud of myself. This year, I do weapons class. I earned a patch by presenting one of my weapons. I earn Certificates of Participation by presenting one of my best Kata—kinds of movement in karate. I go to karate camp to learn more about karate, like to learn the way of the spirit warrior and focusing on the fire of the mind. I meditated every morning at 5:30. I also teach karate to children. I wanted to teach karate because it flows through my mind and body.

I focus on Buddhism because it can clean out my mind and body. The biggest thing I focus on is meditation. Here is my Poem of Meditation:

When we meditate
Then we will light the candles
To let the evil leave us
Then do this meditation with me
To focus deep in your mind and body.
We put the candles around the room
Then relax your mind and body.
The fear does not help you when you cry
But focus on me we will light this candle
To let the bad spirit leave us

For our inner energy
We will practice the spirit warrior
When you focus on me, when you have fear
Then just focus on the fire
Inside of your mind and body
When you are focused on Karate
Then you will do more
Then we will focus on the fire of the heart
If you want the fire just reach deep in your heart.

I am an enlightened Buddha because I believe that death does not end. Life goes on, but life comes to your other world. The darkness and fears go away from your mind and decrease your bad dreams and put good dreams in your mind and body. I don't feel death today because I want no deaths to come, and I want life to come to us and not death. I want life to fill your dreams, to think about in the light of the candles of fire. From now, I learned to meditate, like to pick an object to think about, and I picked karate. It can help me by focusing on the fire of my heart. I have been meditating every day now, and I chant and I focus on the way of the Buddha.

I go to high school, and I have lots of friends like Kathy, Martha, and Nikki. Sometimes, I take the city bus to school. I am learning to drive my dad's jeep, and I am studying for the driving test. School is important to me because I need to learn more skills. I learned PowerPoint and give presentations to the school. At school, I collect cans for money, and the money goes towards a senior trip or a dance. We had a whipped cream fight in the parking lot. I have an education assistant, Floyd, who can help me at school. I love Floyd to work with me.

I am at school to show my trust and my honor and my strength using my mind and body in class. I do the most work, more than the other students do in class. I watch students and what they do like leave trash in the school, and they smoke in the courtyard. I talk at assembly about smoking, how it's bad for the students' health. I did a presentation last year about smoking. I know that my uncle Rob died from smoking, but these students can learn to stop smoking. I also showed these students how we keep the school clean. I have advice for what teachers can do better for the students. Don't push them into work but let the students work harder in their own time.

I already graduated. When I was a senior, I skipped class and went bowling with my classmates. I still go to high school, but I

 also have concurrent enrollment at TVI—a community college in Albuquerque. I have already started wood working and welding class. I have made lots of projects like a folding table, toolbox, and a small chair. I am starting new projects. I love being in wood working because I can become a wood worker. I have lots of friends, like Alex, and I make projects for sale at Santa Fe market. The other things I want to do in TVI is to get into computer class to learn the technology of computers and use PowerPoint.

I make mosaic tables to sell. The steps to make a table are to draw a design, and the next step is to draw it on the table top. Then, you pick the color tile. The next step is to break the tile in small pieces. Then, you glue the tile on and let the glue set for 24 hours. Then, you put the grout on, then wait 24 hours. Then, you put the border on. Then, there is a mosaic table.

I work at Smith's grocery store. I sack bags and carry carts back and forth. I work there for the money. Last year, I saved $100 to go to Telluride for the bluegrass festival. Every year, my family and I go to Telluride Music Festival. The thing that I do around the festival is to ride my bike to the grounds, and I just ride to the mountain. At the grounds, they have a super mall, and there is a food court. My best food is chicken and Coke. My favorite musicians are Sam Bush and Mary Chapin Carpenter. I think the music is the best in the world. Sam Bush plays mandolin, and I am learning to play mandolin.

I like to travel. The places I fly to are Cancun, LA, and Boston. I went on a vacation to Cancun. I rented a bike and a lock, and I ride everywhere I go. I like to go to the beach and swimming in the ocean. I learned to scuba dive, and I went down about 70 feet deep and spent about 1 hour down there. I gambled with a group of girls. I like playing poker. I flew to LA to go to a meditation retreat. We meditate about 5 hours. I also went swimming and shopping in the mall.

The other place I flew to was Boston. I gave a presentation at the TASH conference with my friends and family about my life. Phillip is another student who presented. After the conference, I went with Phillip to lunch and dinner and the mall. We catch the cab to ride to an Ethiopian restaurant. We ate with our hands. We just have lots of fun there. After dinner, we called a cab because it was cold and Phillip uses a wheelchair. No cabs would come. It was too late. As we walked back to the hotel, I saw a cab and hailed one for Phillip. Everyone thought it was cool that I found a cab when everyone else couldn't.

I set my alarm to get up for the gym in the morning at 5:30 A.M. I go to the gym so I can pump iron. I have a trainer named Dornie. She helps me to get strong. That's how I can get fit. My biggest goal is to meet Chuck Norris and Arnold Schwarzenegger, and Jet Li, too. I think that I can be an actor in movies, and I can use my karate skills in the movies.

The other things I want do is to do the Fear Factor TV show. I think that I can eat the guts and bugs and go on the high climbing. I think that I can do Fear Factor. I feel strong and focused. I meditate on breathing techniques. That's the important thing to use when you are scared.

I want to talk about my grandpa's house. I did a lot of things around the house. Like in the bathroom, I took tile off the wall over the bathtub, and I took out the sink and the can. In the front yard, I took out the two tree stumps, and I helped to plant flowers and trees, and I carried a big rock in the front. In the backyard, I dug out a hole for the pond, and I planted roses and flowers, and I put down sod. I carried flagstone for the path, and behind the wood working shop, I am putting a dog run so my dogs can run through. I helped to carry a heavy Buddha in the backyard near the pond. My mom put goldfish in and tadpoles in and plants in the pond. Inside, my dad did the most work, and I went in my new room to clean it out. I am not done yet, so I need to wash the walls, and I am going to paint it the Buddha color and the ocean blue color. I did so much around the house. I can be a landscaper and build houses.

I love my family. Many people have died in my family. My grandpa Proo died. My grandpa died from killing himself with a handgun. I miss him so much. My uncle Rob died from smoking, and my great grandma died. My aunt Helen died, and my uncle Stewart died, and my aunt Mary died, too. There is so much suffering and too many deaths around the world. I meditate on the life and death. I focus on life because there is caring and compassion to others. I want to help defeat the death and sickness around the world.

I will wrap up my chapter, and I think that I did so many things over 18 years because I do so much work and activities in my life and school. My biggest thing I focus on is meditation. Meditation helped me work on my chapter. The parts of my chapter I love most are about karate and Fear Factor. I have many things still to do. Go on my web site on-line some time at http://homepage.mac.com/ vproux50 and look at my movie of me when I was testing for my black belt. Check out my other clips like when I was born and other clips about my life.

I will finish with one more poem. I call this "The Passion of Carson Proo of the Buddha":

The things that I feel
Like feeling no fear
But my spirit is strong
When my body burns
Down in the dirt
That's my soul
I leave my body
From the flesh of my blood
Of my passion
Through my weakness
Through my mind and body
When I wear my crown of thorns
In my mind I have all the blessings
And the compassion that all my friends
My Parents and my grandma
And they all love me so much
That I wanted to die for
I carry my cross through the hall
To the nature of Buddhism
And I want to be a powerful Buddha
To protect my parents
My friends and my Grandma

8

Growing Up with Carson

Victor Proo

We feel that the most important thing we've done for Carson has been to accept him and have high expectations for him with no exceptions—and to expect others to accept him and have high expectations for him, too! I tell him all of the time how much we love him and how we, as his parents, are here to help him understand how to get along in the world. We apologize to him when we get angry at him and explain why anger is just an expression of our fears. We always encourage him to be appropriate, even when others are not. We take him with us *everywhere* we go and let him do everything we do: ski; go to the gym; exercise; eat out at restaurants; and go to movies, festivals, dinners, parties, and Temple.

We talk to him—a lot. We always speak normally to him, just the way we do to anyone else. We look him in the eyes—see his wonderful, innocent soul—and treat him like a spiritual human being, a "Clown of God" worthy of love, affection, and respect. We let him know that he *is* a special/different *person* with Down syndrome, and that is perfectly okay—normal!

An important thing, I think, we did in the beginning was to use positive reinforcement and redirection when he would do, or look like he was going to do, something potentially harmful or dangerous and then *praise* him to the "Nth" degree for his correct decisions—*all* of the time. One grade school teacher once told us, "He has too much self-esteem!" We told her that we believed there would be enough people in the world who would try to knock him down a few notches, so the higher his self-esteem, the more difficult to knock him down too far. He just gets up and keeps right on going!

Our intention with his appearance has always been to allow him to express himself but to try to help him to do it with some dignity. We feel that we are allowing him to express himself at an early age when it is less likely to affect a job or career. In the future, he will have already experimented with different looks and styles.

His clothing style is a direct manifestation of his lovely mother's great sense of current-day *cool*! She helps him pick out all of his clothes—mine, too, thank goodness. If it were left to me alone, God help him! Susie just has a talent for knowing what other kids will find acceptable and cool in his age range. It just helps him fit in at school and around here in our part of the country.

Carson's elementary and middle school years were all in special needs classrooms, self-contained but supposedly inclusive with areas like lunch and art. During the elementary years, we did not mind this, as we felt it was a safe environment for him. But by middle and high school, we felt that he was ready to be more and more included in regular education classes. High school has been a great period of growth and exploration for him, us, and his school teachers and classmates. He has been enrolled in a charter high school with teachers who were greatly interested in expanding the high school environment of their students to include community service for all students. Understanding people of all kinds was high on their list of learning experiences, so having someone like Carson in their midst has given them "a real sense of what it means to be someone with a disability and what the true meaning of compassion is!" This is a direct quote from the principal and founder of the school.

Carson started Special Olympics at about the age of 13. It was our intention to expand his social circle and see if he couldn't find some friends there, but, alas, that was not to be the case. He was still alone, and no one really clicked with him or vice versa. He started karate at the age of 9, and he took to it like a bird in flight. As the web site http://homepage.mac.com/vproux50 attests, he has achieved his black belt after 10 years of hard work, training, and never giving up. He truly loves the martial arts and will do anything to continue. He is now doing weapons training with bows, staffs, and swords. Carson has a couple of friends who he has had the unique opportunity to spend time with. Sleepovers, camping, movies, playing ... but otherwise it has been hard, and we understand the frustration and heartbreak some parents experience with regard to the aloneness of their children.

We enjoy nurturing relationships with people from around the country and world as a result of Carson's web site. Who knows when we might actually get our children together in the future and what they might accomplish?

II

Friendships
and Support

9

Who's That Girl?

Farrah Hernton

While I was brainstorming about what to write for this chapter, I encountered a little dilemma. I usually do really well when it comes to discussing other topics, but when I was asked to write this chapter about myself, I was a little more than hesitant. I kept thinking to myself, "What on earth could I possibly have to write about"? Then, I began thinking I actually have been through a lot of things in my life, and it might be good to talk about some of those experiences. So, in this, I will tell about my experiences in and outside of school and how those experiences have affected me.

I have to say that from the very beginning of things, I felt I was at an obvious disadvantage. When I was at the age of 2, my parents discovered that something was wrong. That is when the doctor explained to them that I had a disability called cerebral palsy. My parents have told me they were shocked to find this out because they felt they should have been told earlier.

Early on in my childhood, I did not really feel any different from any other child. Now that I look back on it, I believe that the only reason I did not think too much about my disability at this time was because I was just a little girl. I was more concerned with combing my babydoll's hair. As I reflect back on this and all that has taken place since then, sometimes I wish I could return to this much simpler time. I was just cheerful and naïve. My family had treated me as though there was no difference between my brothers and me. I think that is part of the reason that I was so unprepared for what I was to experience later on when I started school.

I really find it hard to explain what it was like for me during those early years of school. I think that is when I was really forced to realize that no matter how much I wanted to be or thought I was like everyone else, I really was going to be looked at as different. I think it was during my elementary school years that I became confused and upset about being born with a disability. I recall being in this one particular special education class from kindergarten all the way through third grade. It was a class for the most severe disabilities in the school, where we never went into general education classes. It is hard for me to imagine, now having been in a regular classroom environment, given how far I have come from elementary school. At first, it used to bother me too much being in there. But after a while, I began to just feel frustrated. I was in there with kids who could barely function. I just remember coming home and telling my parents that I do not belong in there. The work was too easy. Although I liked coming home with no homework, that class just really bothered me. I felt we had no interaction with other students. We were not even allowed to eat our lunch in the cafeteria; it had to be brought to us. This is just one example of the bad experiences I had during my years at school.

I think if I had to describe 1 year that I thought I had the worse teacher ever, it would have to be when I was in the fourth grade in Texas. This lady was a complete jerk. Usually, I would not think to talk about teachers like that, but I just do not think there is a word more fitting to describe her. This was my first time ever being placed into a regular ed. class. She was my math teacher.

There are several reasons why I did not like her. One reason was because I don't think she could teach well. Another reason is because I believe she was prejudiced against me. I would go inside the classroom, and it was like a nightmare. I would ask her a question, and she would just completely broadcast the fact that I didn't know what I was doing instead of helping me in private.

I remember one horrible incident vividly. I came to class this particular day, and my homework was not finished. I explained to her that it was because there were too many problems and I did not quite understand how to do it. All of a sudden, her face got very red, and she screamed at me, "I knew you did not belong here.

People like you cannot do this type of work!" I was absolutely mortified. She had yelled at me before, but this time was quite different. I could see the hatred in her eyes. I also heard the other students laughing in the background.

When I came home from school that day, I was devastated, and for a while I stopped doing any of my homework. I stopped wanting to go to school at all. Finally, one day my dad said to me, "You don't have to let your disability determine who you are and all of what you are capable of." From that day on, I made it my mission not to allow people to tell me what I could or could not do. I wanted to prove to this particular teacher and other individuals who had said mean and cruel things to me that they were wrong. I did end up passing that particular class despite my frustrations.

Now that I think back on all my years of school, not including my senior year of high school, I do not believe any of it was too enjoyable. I think that maybe part of the reason for that was because I felt so sheltered. Although I never had an educational assistant until I moved to New Mexico, I still felt I was not totally independent in my other schools. As a matter of fact, I think it was worse because I felt even more out of touch with the students who were in regular classes. Most of the day, we special ed. students stayed secluded in our own little rooms.

What bothers me the most about having been in a setting like that is that numerous teachers and other adults think this is good for students like us. I, still to this day, cannot understand why keeping a small group of students separated away from their nondisabled peers is supposed to be good for them. I believe it makes it difficult for people in special ed. to interact with those who are not. You get so used to seeing and talking to the same few people all day long. I also think being in special ed. sometimes lowers a person's self-esteem.

I cannot speak for everyone who has been in special ed., but it has been hard for me. First, I am very shy, and second, I have a physical disability, which might make people a little hesitant to approach me. I am also a little apprehensive around certain people because it is hard for me to tell whether they are being nice to me because they see me as a cool person, or if they are being nice to me because they feel sorry for me.

I believe that students like Phillip and me are proof that an individual with a disability can succeed in a regular education setting. I believe that all it takes is a teacher to be willing to make a few accommodations for us. It really upsets me when I hear people say regular ed. teachers do not have the time or ability to assist students with disabilities. I refuse to believe this because this year I have learned that there are teachers and students who are willing to accept disabled students.

I have to say that this year, my senior year, has been by far my favorite. It has also been quite an eye-opening experience. I think the reason this year has been my favorite is because of my humanities class. For the first time, I feel that I have been able to sort of become more outgoing and stop being so afraid of how people will react to me because I have a disability. I have also been able to meet some wonderful friends who were willing to endure a struggle just so they could take me to lunch with them.

I have also come to realize that I can succeed in the outside world, where there is no different place set aside for people with disabilities. After all, there is no special ed. McDonalds. I know I will have to overcome a lot of obstacles in the future, but my only wish is to impact as many lives as possible to let the people who are considered "normal" know that there is no difference between me and you . . . except the fact that I get to drive in a speedy wheelchair. All you have to do is open your eyes and see who I really am.

10

Taking Farrah to Lunch

Michelle Murray

Hate crimes, prejudice, and *discrimination* are words you think of when you look back in history. Those are not words commonly used in the year 2003, or are they? The words may not be heard as often, but the actions behind them are still clearly present in our environment. Discriminating against people because of their physical disabilities seems to me to be the worst type of discrimination. It denies all of us the ability to nurture friendships.

In my senior year of high school, I have made a new very close friend who just happens to be in a wheelchair. I had never seen this girl for the 3 previous years that we both have attended the same high school. At the beginning of the semester, Farrah showed up in my senior humanities class. Where had she been? I wondered. Her huge electric chair was not easy to miss, especially in the crowded halls of our overcrowded school.

As we got to know each other better, she and I discussed our experiences at our high school. I found out there was another "world" behind the main building where a collection of portable classrooms defined the boundaries for many students with disabilities. It was as if she and I had attended school in different hemispheres. My outrage was tempered by her courage and strength. She developed a fierce determination to overcome the obstacles that were put in her path because of her disability. She told me stories about students and teachers who had been mean and hateful to her just because she is in a wheelchair.

During a recent fire drill, we became aware of the contrast between Farrah's respectful behavior and the rudeness of others. Not one student or teacher from any other class paused to let us pass or held the door for us. Fortunately, the students in our humanities class were gracious and efficient in helping us evacuate the building. When we returned to the classroom, we discussed our experience. Our teacher, who had been walking with another student who is in a wheelchair, remarked that a fellow teacher pushed his way in front of the chair in order to go through the door first. Needless to say, in his self-centered hurry, he didn't pause to hold the door open behind him. Our class was able to talk openly about the unfair treatment of our classmates with disabilities, whom we had just recently met and were just beginning to recognize as friends. Disabled and nondisabled students alike—we were all in this together.

As a class, we conducted accessibility surveys and disability simulations to understand our school environment a little better. Some of the places where we liked to hang out were unavailable to some of our friends because their wheelchairs couldn't make it through narrow spaces, or over rough terrain, or up a short flight of steps. Even the snack bar counters were too high for a kid in a wheelchair to order a slice of pizza and a soda.

Our close circle of friends now included two other students, Aimee and Abby. Together with Farrah and me, they recognized the often hidden prejudice against a student with a physical disability. Some people seemed to express the idea that just because Farrah was in a wheelchair she couldn't be a "normal" teenager. One incident in particular of not-so-subtle segregation stands out in my mind. It occurred about 2 months into our senior year. Surprisingly, or maybe not, it involved teachers and administrators, not students.

Our high school campus is closed except for seniors. For our first 3 years of high school, we were relegated to the school cafeteria or whatever areas of the commons that we could claim. Leaving campus for lunch was, we felt, a hard-earned privilege, one that we cherished and would not give up without a fight. Farrah earned that privilege, too; yet, she had not been able to join us for lunch because of the difficulties with transporting her wheelchair.

We thought we would fix that and decided to take Farrah to lunch with us.

Our teacher thought it was a great idea and helped to arrange an activity-related excused absence for the periods just before and after lunch so that we could take the time we needed to take care of transportation. Farrah suggested that she could bring her manual wheelchair to school because it is lighter and easier to transport. We all talked to Farrah's parents and received their permission for Farrah to leave campus during the lunch period. We made arrangements with each other and with some of our friends to get Farrah and her wheelchair into and out of one of our vehicles. Because we would be leaving early, our teacher suggested that we should check with administration before we were stopped at the gate and prevented from carrying out our plan.

The four of us, Aimee, Abby, Farrah, and me, followed her advice—although we would regret it later. We started at the bottom of the chain of command with Farrah's support teacher. To say the least, she was not thrilled with the idea at all. She told us there was too much liability and too many hazards in three girls' lifting a "wheelchair-bound" girl into a truck. We listened politely and left her office. We were determined to win this battle and would not be put off by the first obstacle we encountered.

We took another step up in the administrative chain. We marched and wheeled into the office of the head teacher of the special education department. (We, of course, thought it was kind of silly that Farrah is in special ed. because of her disability. She is smarter than most of our class.) Ms. Jones said there was a "slim-to-none" chance of our being able to accomplish what we set out to do. We would need a lift to get her into the truck properly. We looked at her and reminded her that many of our friends are football players. After a bit of persuading, we were able to convince her to reconsider our chances. Farrah would bring in a written note from her parents giving us permission to take her off campus and releasing the school of any liability. Ms. Jones said she would take it to her boss, the school principal, once we brought in the letter.

Farrah, like most of us, does not always remember to bring paperwork to school. In this case, it was the parent permission form and not homework. Eventually, however, the note appeared in her backpack, and we headed back down to the special education office. The head of the department was walking toward the main office when we caught up with her. She again warned us that we might still be disappointed, that we should "just remember [the note] doesn't mean that you are going to be able to do this."

We walked toward one of the assistant principals, and, in passing, Ms. Jones mentioned what we planned to do. He stopped dead in his tracks, looked at the four of us, and took the letter out of our hands. We waited anxiously for his reaction as he read the note. He looked back at us, and suddenly a smile brightened his face. To our delight, he said, "This is a great idea. You should be all set to go. We'll put this in her file so we have it if we need it. Go. Have fun!" At last, we were set to go. We had permission from her parents, our teacher, the head of the special education department, and now our administration. We were ready to rock.

Looking back at our determined fight, we realize how important it was for us to get some time together outside of the school building. We needed to talk about "girl stuff." The trips back and forth to lunch helped us to get better at transferring Farrah and loading and unloading her chair. Each outing became easier—and more fun. Four girls out at lunch during the school day was a dream come true. In fact, some of our other, nondisabled friends wanted to join us. Ordinarily we would have said, "Come on," but this time was too special to us. It was ours alone. Our friendship grew deeper and more steady. Aimee, Abby, and I had jobs after school, so our lunchtimes became more and more precious to us. We really valued every minute we could just hang out together.

Farrah came with us to our senior "play day." The senior class met at a local outdoor sports complex to be silly, have lunch, and just spend time together with our classmates in one of the last days before we graduated and moved on. Having learned how to operate in the system, we politely approached the activities director and asked if there would be a wheelchair-accessible bus so that Farrah could join her classmates. She thanked us for reminding her and immediately called the bus company to change the original reservations. I think we were all a little surprised; we had expected some resistance.

There was only one drawback to the day's activities. The area where lunch was served was not accessible for Farrah's wheelchair. That posed no problem at all to us now. Three boys hefted the heavy, motorized wheelchair down some stairs. One of the wrestlers carried Farrah to his table, and the fun continued. The meal was followed by water balloons and shaving cream. Farrah was just as messy as the rest of us when we were ready to head home.

Now that this is all behind us, it seems like a happy story with a happy ending. But if you look at it from a different angle, it seems a little less straightforward. It all started when four girls wanted to go to lunch together. You have to wonder why there was so much red tape. Why were the rules different for a disabled student than for typical students? Wasn't this discrimination? If you ask any one of the four of us, we'd say, "Of course!" The administration thought that they were helping Farrah by trying to protect her; they believed they had her best interest in mind throughout it all. In actuality, they were stifling her independence and building additional barriers that prevented her from being more independent.

With determination and passion in our hearts, we fought—and beat—the system. We set a path for others to follow, just by taking Farrah to lunch.

11

"We Don't Need a Wheelchair Lift . . . We Have Football Players"

Transformational Experiences in Inclusive Education

Sherry Jones

As a teacher, I've always taken pride in providing the best services available for individuals with disabilities. I would constantly strive to implement research-based practices for my students in special education. Whether I was teaching vocational skills or providing academic remediation to my high school students, I felt that I was giving them exactly what they needed to be happy, productive members of the community. I used to teach kids with similar disabilities together in one room out in the portables. I figured that by keeping them together I could teach them the skills they so desperately needed. I was also in a better position to protect them from the possible dangers inherent in a large, overcrowded high school.

Now, my views about students and services have changed dramatically. I realized that we can learn so much about making the educational experience more meaningful for students if we listen to them and include their input in challenging situations. I have to contribute this new view on education to three inspirational individuals—Ellen, Charlotte, and Michelle.

Ellen was one of my students in my self-contained special education class several years ago. Although Ellen had difficulties in written language, I quickly realized that she had strengths in math. "I'm bored. Can't we do some harder math?" she asked me one day. Ellen craved more academic challenges, but I knew that I couldn't help her reach her full academic potential by myself. I went to a math teacher I respected and asked his advice. We decided that she would attend the general ed. class for lectures, then leave the class and return to my room for the standard drill and practice.

Despite best intentions, this plan was disastrous and frustrated Ellen immensely. Now, not only was the work harder, but she also had to endure two teachers with different styles and expectations telling her what to do. After weeks of struggling, she burst into my room sobbing. "Please don't make me go back there, Miss Jones," she pleaded. I looked at her quizzically. She further explained, "I can't do the work. All the other kids seem to know what they're doing in there except me." My first inclination was to pull her out of the class. When I saw the tears stream down her face, I felt compelled to protect her. I had to save her self-esteem, and the best way to do that was to keep her with me. Even though she wouldn't be challenged, I knew she would feel safe and that would make her happy. I made my decision to pull her back into my class.

I went home that evening with the events of the day on my mind and did some soul searching. Something inside me told me I was handling this situation all wrong. I cared so much about Ellen, and her tears broke my heart. I knew she needed more challenges than I could provide in my class, but I was afraid to let her go. I replayed our conversation over and over in my mind. After hours of analysis, I realized that there had to be a better way to fix Ellen's problem other than pulling her back into the small-group setting. The next day, I spent the morning with her math teacher. We talked and came to understand that that we weren't giving Ellen the support she needed.

The classroom learning didn't occur during the lecture, but rather during the activities that ensued. Mastery of the curriculum was a product of the time the students spent together with guidance from the teacher. Ellen's frustration wasn't because she was spending too much time in general education. On the contrary, she wasn't spending enough time with her peers.

I encouraged Ellen to go back to the class. At first, she fought me. "No way, Miss Jones. I hate it in there," she told me. I told her that this time it would be different. I explained that the teachers figured out what went wrong, and this time we knew how to fix it.

Grudgingly, she went back. This time, however, she remained in the room for the entire period. The other students welcomed her into their study groups. I saw relationships develop between Ellen and several other students, and she became a true member of the classroom community. The kids in the class figured out how to make her feel included and welcome. Amazingly, she flourished both academically and socially. This was a testament that a special education label does not preclude learning. I learned that with accommodations and support any kid can be successful.

I have since moved from the classroom to an administrative position. For the past 8 years, I have had the privilege of overseeing the special education program at my school. I believe that we harbor some of the most progressive special education programs in the state. These innovative programs were initiated by a true visionary in the field, Charlotte Mullins.

"Char" was the previous special education chairperson who found positive attributes in all students. She challenged us as a staff to provide meaningful opportunities for students with disabilities. She frequently informed us about the value of listening to the students in our classes. It was not uncommon to see kids stopping by to visit "Mrs. Mullins." She welcomed input from students about the types of support they needed to be successful, and her actions were constant reminders of how important it was for us to do the same. She encouraged us to take risks and grow as educators. Her passion for students was infectious, and her guidance and support changed many lives.

Char motivated her staff to try new, sometimes unconventional, ideas and then eventually turned the reigns over to me. I was thrilled about the prospect of supervising the largest special education staff in the state of New Mexico. I only hoped I could be as imaginative and inspiring a leader as my predecessor. Char fully endorsed the concept of inclusion, and I was determined to uphold her legacy.

Indeed, our inclusion program for students with mild disabilities was blossoming; however, students with moderate or significant disabilities were still being segregated. This section of our school population was not visible on campus. They were rarely in the hallways. They didn't ride the same buses as the other students, they didn't have lockers, and they didn't have the same books or teachers as any of the "regular" kids. For the most part, they attended a school within in a school.

Although I encouraged placing the kids with mild disabilities in general education for most if not all of the day, I wasn't sold on the idea of including the kids with more significant needs in this endeavor. How could general education possibly benefit "these" kids? What if other students teased or exploited them? How could they make friends? I was extremely hesitant about the impact of inclusion on the students without disabilities until I met Michelle.

I was sitting in my office when I heard the commotion. I got up and greeted the group of high school seniors waiting impatiently for my attention. "What can I do for you, girls?" I asked.

Michelle, the spokesperson for the group, answered, "We want to take Farrah off campus to lunch. We were told we can't do that without talking to you. Why?"

The first thing that went through my mind was how can they possibly do this? Farrah uses a wheelchair. Don't they know how hard it would be to get her off campus? Farrah is supposed to have a paraprofessional with her when she's at school to help her in her classes. I asked, "Well, is her educational assistant going with you?"

They looked at me as if I was crazy. "No," Michelle replied, sounding almost hostile. "Why does *she* need to go with us?"

In fear of violating the individualized education program (IEP) and the potential of putting Farrah at risk by allowing her off campus without adult support, I became a typical bureaucrat. "First," I began, "you need to get written parent approval. Then, you must give me a plan explaining how you are going to pay for the special ed. bus to transport her." I was hoping to buy some time to look into the legalities of letting this child in a wheelchair leave school unsupervised.

Michelle looked perplexed. "I don't understand what the problem is," she retorted. "This is an open campus. No other senior needs a note to leave. She needs to have a senior experience just like everyone else."

Not to sound callous or unsympathetic, I responded, "I can appreciate that, but there are rules I must follow. You need to do what I ask before I even consider letting her leave campus."

Michelle's mouth dropped in disbelief at the perceived ridiculousness of my request. After all, they were seniors at a school with an open campus. The girls stormed out. I figured I put an end to this shenanigan. Little did I know, but this was not the end of the fight to get Farrah off campus. Soon after, I ran into the girls in the hallway. Michelle handed me the parent approval with a smile. "Here it is, Miss Jones. Can we go now?"

I glanced at the paper. "I'm glad you got permission, but that's just the first step. She needs a wheelchair lift. How are you going to pay for the bus to transport her?" I asked.

She stared at me for a moment. "Why do we need a wheelchair lift? We have football players!" she responded with a self-satisfied smirk.

I began to chuckle and recognized the absurdity of all the bureaucratic red tape I was making the girls wade through. "Of course," I mused, "football players . . . why didn't I think of that?" The students found an easy solution to a problem that was I was creating. I decided they had proved their point. I was wrong, and they needed my support and encouragement with the principal.

As we made our way to the administrative offices, I cautioned the girls that they hadn't won the battle yet. Although I backed them, I wasn't sure about the administration's view on potential legal difficulties associated with this scenario. I walked the girls in to see the principal, and they explained their plight. The principal reviewed the letter from Farrah's parents and looked at me to see my reaction. When he saw me smile and nod my head in approval, he turned toward Michelle and shrugged his shoulders. "I can't see why this should be problem. Have a good time, girls," he chirped. They beamed and scurried away.

The experiences with Ellen, Charlotte, and Michelle altered my views on the power of inclusion and its impact on students with and without disabilities. Often, perceived barriers are not real barriers at all. They're contrived by well-meaning professionals. In an attempt to act in the best interest of kids with disabilities, we inadvertently exclude them from having normal experiences. Sometimes, the solution is so simple, but the adults overanalyze the problem. We limit independence and opportunities for relationships to occur by putting up obstacles that are manufactured from our own fears. When students are left to their own means, they provide the avenues for friendships to develop in ways that we, the adults, would never imagine.

Inclusive education is more than merely providing academic support to students with disabilities. Rather, it is a humanitarian benefit to society that includes and acknowledges diversity in all of its forms. Inclusion, like all social change, requires planning, training, and the ability to embrace new ideas. It is essential that students are included in this process because they are the ones who provide the greatest guidance. They are the ones with the answers. They are the ones who can make the seemingly impossible become a reality.

12

One Look, One Smile, and Two People

Erin Pitcher

I can't remember exactly everyone I saw when I entered the room. I can't remember exactly where I sat, but I can remember the fear that I felt when I walked into the classroom, and I can remember feeling like *I* was out of place. I can remember a boy in a wheelchair who sat by the door because there was no room to move around in the back of the room. He was blond, blue eyed, and had a beautiful smile. The only thing was that he didn't seem to talk. He was kind of spastic and drooled a lot, I thought.

He intrigued me, though. I couldn't stop watching him. Why couldn't he talk? What is wrong with him? Should I go sit by him? Is he nice? All I knew is that I had to get to know him.

The next couple of days went by, and I started sitting by this boy. I found out his name was David. I started taking his notes for him since he couldn't write. I told him my name and tried talking to him a lot. He was kind of shy. He would smile and look away sweetly. I didn't know if David understood me. I didn't even know if he knew I was talking to him, but I still persisted on talking to him.

Weeks went by, and David and I grew to be friends. He recognized me right away whenever I saw him, and he smiled at me a lot. I started watching his motions and the way his eyes shifted so that I could try to understand what he was trying to say. It seemed as if one day it just clicked; I knew what he was saying. I can remember David and I working on a brain project, and I asked him if he liked the brain and why. He told me that he liked the brain because it was gross looking. He told me all of that just by pointing at a picture of a brain and nodding while sticking his tongue out to show me it was gross. I was so excited that he and I had finally communicated.

During the whole project I had been stressing about how to incorporate David into it so that he could participate, and then it finally came to me. If I could somehow have David point to different parts of the brain while I was presenting, I would have incorporated him and have had him learn something as well. Later on that same evening, I was drawing a large picture of a brain on a poster board and coloring in the different lobes on the brain. Each lobe was a different color. As I was finishing, I thought of a way to make it even better for David. I decided to cut out different lobes and color them according to the lobes on the poster and attach Velcro to the backs of the lobes so that David could stick the different lobes on the poster as I was presenting.

The next day, our presentation was a hit. David and I had accomplished things that it took some people the rest of the year to accomplish. David and I had communicated on a deeper level and worked together to accomplish a goal and learn something at the same time. This is what inclusion education is all about.

David and I sat together every day the entire school year. We did every project and presentation together. I met him every day in the morning when the buses dropped him off at school. I even went and visited David many times while he was in the hospital and at home recovering from his surgery.

David and I grew the closest when I visited him the day after surgery in the hospital. He had had major surgery that had to be done immediately. I remember walking into his recovery room with a huge poster that said, "Get Well Soon, David!" and a stuffed animal horse (horses are his favorite animal because his grandma has one). I also had a picture of me so that he knew that I was always with him in my prayers and thoughts.

As I walked into the room, I wasn't quite prepared for what I was about to see. David was propped up in his bed. He was crying, exhausted, and in a lot of pain. I'll never forget the moaning sounds he made; it struck me to my core. I said hi to him and smiled, trying to be as happy as I could be. I was holding back from crying, and I'm sure he could tell.

I walked over to where he could see me. He recognized me and immediately stopped crying and moaning. He smiled at me—It was a moment I'll never forget. I knew that me being there made his day and touched him. I knew that David really admired me, so I knew that me being there was special for him. That day, I saw David in a different way. It was as if I was supposed to see him that way so that we could be closer. I'm so glad that that day happened.

The next day when I visited him, I walked into the room again expecting him not to be well again, but there was David, watching cartoons (SpongeBob, his favorite) and snuggling the stuffed animal I got him. He was so excited to see me. He pointed to the wall where his mom and grandma had hung up the poster that I made him. David then pointed to the rail on his bed, and there was my picture. He smiled at me and tried to give me kisses on my head when I had to leave. David's spirit amazed me. Even when he was in pain, he put the pain aside just to make someone happy.

David still amazes me to this day. Every day, David teaches me how to be a better person. The couple of weeks that he was in the hospital made me realize that working with kids with disabilities is what I want to do for the rest of my life. Working with David has fulfilled me in a way that no good grade on a test or being the best cheerleader ever has. When I leave my classroom each day, I feel happy and satisfied. I feel like I have done something to improve someone else's life. I feel like I finally found who I am and why I am here.

David's and my relationship is unusual. Sure, general ed. kids and special ed. kids have been friends before, but not on the same level as David and me. Some teachers looking into inclusion education are afraid that the special ed. kids and the general ed. kids won't mix, but the truth is that they will with the attitude of the students themselves and the teacher. People in my inclusive class sometimes ask me how I know what David is saying and how I'm not afraid of him. I tell them that I just look into his eyes and watch what he is doing. Sometimes, saying nothing at all says the most. When they ask how I'm not afraid of him I think, "How can people think people with disabilities are scary and that they have to be afraid?" I think its because of ignorance, a lack of understanding the disabilities.

I admit, in the beginning of the year I was afraid, but that's because *I* was ignorant. I had no clue about kids with disabilities or inclusion. How are people supposed to understand and mix with kids with disabilities if the kids with disabilities are put in portables in the back of the school like so many schools do? How are teachers supposed to have the right attitude about inclusion if they've never been around kids with disabilities themselves? These are the types of questions you have to ask yourself when thinking about inclusion. Inclusion works, but the only way is if people are educated about disabilities and immersed in a setting with both kids with disabilities and kids without disabilities.

When I say educated, I mean *aware* of disabilities. I remember when I first started my inclusion class, no one knew who had what kind of disability or even who had a disability at all. To me, this was the best thing that my teachers could have done. It wasn't important to know who had a disability. We were just any other class with different people all coming together as one whole. I never knew what disability David had until the class did the brain project and I watched a group's video about disabilities. I was shocked when I saw David on the screen. I didn't know that he had that disability, but that didn't matter to me because I had already gotten to know David beyond his disability. This is another thing that inclusion does; it lets people get to know other people beyond their disability.

The things that I have learned from my inclusion class are invaluable to me and have impacted me in a way that I don't think anything else would have. David is the biggest thing that has impacted my life, but also speaking to other people about inclusion education has impacted me in a different sort of way.

I have always been a chatty, outgoing person, so I thought it was no big deal when my teacher, Dr. Moore, asked me if I would speak to some graduate students at UNM (University of New Mexico) about my inclusion class. When I got to the classroom along with some classmates of mine, I casually sat down in front of the class of about 20 or so and smiled waiting for our turn to talk. I started talking first about my experience with my inclusion class and what I liked and disliked. That was the easy part. Soon afterwards, there were tons of questions, some irritating because they were asked over and over, and some that made me think.

One of those questions was, "How has inclusion impacted you?" At first, I thought that the answer was simple; it has made me a better person. Then, I began to think deeper. It hasn't just made me a better person, its changed the way I view other people. It's changed my career goals. It's made me a more patient and understanding person. It's made the real Erin shine through. It made me be more mature than other people because I was immersed in more difficult situations than other high schoolers.

I was suddenly not interested in who is going to prom with whom; I was interested in issues such as are there ramps for the kids in wheelchairs to go up? Is the door wide enough for David to fit through with his chair? Sitting there in front of that class, I realized that I have grown up. Inclusion has given me the opportunity to find myself and find invaluable skills that will help me for the rest of my life.

For a long while, I have wanted to be a prosecution attorney. I thought it would be fun to be a lawyer and fight for the good of the people. Then, I took my inclusion class, communication skills in action. Working with David and being around kids with disabilities has changed my career idea from being a prosecution attorney to a special needs advocate and a dual licensed teacher with a Ph.D. so that I am able to teach high school students. I have realized that being in the inclusion setting and working with kids with disabilities is what I am passionate about, and I want to share my passion with other people. To me, I feel that society doesn't really, truly accept people with disabilities and really doesn't like the idea of kids with disabilities learning in the same classroom with general ed. kids. I want to be an inclusion teacher to help change the way society views people with disabilities.

Just recently I spoke at the Second Annual Quality Education Least Restrictive Environment Summer Institute in my hometown. My first appearance was in front of a "strand" in a conference room. A "strand" is a group of people from the area or region you are from. I walked into the conference room with three other classmates, and we all sat down. It was a comfortable setting with about 20–30 people, just like a UNM class. The other classmates and I started giving our same spiel that we always did about our experience in inclusion, but something about this group of people that we were speaking to was different from the rest. Some people really understood what we were saying; others politely took notes but asked us questions that a lot of other people had never asked. Afterward, my classmates and I found out from our teachers, who were in charge of that particular strand, that the group of people consisted of teachers, parents, and people interested in the inclusion setting.

After my classmates and I talked to the "strand" group assigned to us, my teachers asked me if I would be willing to talk in front of the whole conference about my experience in inclusion. I told them that I could, even though I knew there were going to be about 400 people that I would be speaking to. After they asked me, I never really thought twice about it. I wasn't nervous or scared or intimidated. That's when I realized that speaking to people about inclusion is my calling.

Three days later, I arrived at the conference again to speak in front of the whole conference. I knew that two other people who had disabilities were going to speak in front of the whole conference with me. I waited with my teachers for the two people to show up, but after waiting 20 or 30 minutes, only one showed. The young man who showed up had graduated from our high school 1 or 2 years ago and had dyslexia. I couldn't tell that he had anything. When we stood on the podium together, he spoke with such confidence and poise and professionalism that it took me back.

When we spoke, there was a certain order that we did things in. First, he spoke, then I. Second, there were 10 questions. Third, there was only 20–25 minutes for both of us to speak. The alternation between he and I was amazing. It was interesting and intriguing to see first a special ed. student's opinion then to see a general ed. student's opinion. It was like night and day when we spoke about inclusion and special ed. I think that speaking to that many people was a great way of advocating and advertising inclusion. I think it is good for kids, classmates, teachers, and parents to see how kids with or without disabilities can work together in an inclusion class and those kids who are left in special ed. do sometimes really want to be included just like everyone else.

Summer has come and gone, and the starting of the new school year has been absolutely crazy. David and I are taking science together plus a peer buddies class. Starting science with David has been very challenging but well worth my while. At first, I thought I knew how to work with David well ... in communication skills class, yes, but science, well that was a different story. It has been hard trying to find what works best for David in the new and more challenging setting. It has also been hard trying to balance class time with David time. The corks and screws are still being worked out, but every day that I am allowed to work with David is a gift that I treasure. It is a very special thing to say that everyday I learn a thousand new things from David, but it is true, and everything I have experienced has been very rewarding.

As I think back to the day that I first saw David, approximately 1 year ago, its hard to think that he and his love could have brought me this far. The opportunities that inclusion has opened for me is overwhelming, and I am truly blessed to have been in an inclusion program that has worked so well for so many different people. It is mind boggling to think that all this that I have shared started by one look, one smile, and two people who were open to all the possibilities in the world, and look how far it has brought us.

13

This Is Why!

Heather Curran

My name is Heather Curran, and I am 15 years old. I'm a tenth grader in high school. I love to watch TV, and I like riding horses. I am a cheerleader on the JV (junior varsity) squad.

Here at school, I have six classes: Spanish, geometry, photography, geology, English, and communication skills in action. I usually do the day-to-day things in most of my classes, such as notes, lectures, and worksheets. School, at times, can be easy, but for the most part, it's pretty tough for me. It's hard for me to remember things when all the teachers do is lecture, or dictate notes, or hand out worksheets. I learn better visually and by hands-on activities, but I just have gotten used to expecting lectures and routine assignments. For example, in my geology class, we know what we are doing every day because it is always the same thing, over and over again. It gets old and loses my attention.

The best part about school is getting to see my friends every day, meeting new people, and learning things I never knew before. What helps me a lot at school is when I can tell that the teachers are excited and love what they do because then they try to make the class interesting—like my first period class: communication skills in action. My teachers in this class love what they do, and we can tell that they do. It's my favorite class. The teachers make it interesting by changing the way they teach every day. One day, they might give us a group activity, and then, on another day, they might give us information in a lecture with notes on the board or overhead. That's what makes school more enjoyable.

The worst part of school, I would say, is not understanding. This is the worst for me because sometimes, no matter how many times a teacher tells me something, I still may not get it. Often, I have to go to another teacher or classmate for extra help and have it explained to me another way. It makes school hard. I'm there for 8 hours every day, and I feel that I can't learn because I can't get it all, and it doesn't make sense. The day can seem very long and frustrating.

It might sound funny, but what also makes school bad is the atmosphere. If a room has an uncomfortable feeling for me, it is hard for me to concentrate. One of my worst memories is from a class in middle school. Some students made fun of me, and it ruined the whole year. It was hard for me to study or concentrate on my work. It really made me depressed, and my self-esteem was low. When I came to high school, though, it completely changed.

As I said before, my first period class this year is communication skills in action. It's just like a regular communication skills class, but we also have some classmates with special needs who are with us every day. This class is different from other classes I have been in. The kids with special needs have usually been out in the portables. We do a lot of group activities. One of our group projects was on ADHD (attention-deficit/hyperactivity disorder). Everyone in the group participated in the work and in the class presentation.

We also do individual projects. We are working on one now. It is a letter to our pen pals in the third grade. We learn to write formal letters but in a way that is fun. Besides, we have to think about what we can write that will be interesting to third graders and is not just about ourselves. We are able to visit our pen pals because the elementary school is just up the street. We all walk there together as a field trip with our teachers.

The first time I walked into my communication skills class, I was intimidated by the kids with special needs in the class. I didn't know how to act or treat them or what they would think or do. I was scared and nervous. I really wanted to meet them, but I didn't know what to say. The teachers helped us to meet each other by putting us into groups to work on activities together. It really helped that the teachers organized the groups and were there to answer questions and to help us solve our problems and to give us advice. Little by little, I got to know all of my classmates and started to make new friends.

To me, inclusion means to include everyone, no matter what, and to treat everyone fairly. I can't stress enough that inclusion is so important. There are kids in my class now that have never before been in a class with more than eight students. They never had the chance to be in a regular class. I met a kid named Chad this year. We went to the same middle school and never even saw each other. This is why I believe inclusion is so important. It's not fair to exclude kids just because they may need more help than other students.

Teachers can start in elementary school and encourage the kids to include everyone. Teachers can also put kids with special needs in their classes. It's not fair to me or to them that we couldn't know each other in elementary or middle school. If the schools started inclusion earlier and kept it going through middle school, it would change the way kids treat each other.

This class has changed me in so many ways. For one, I am not afraid to meet or talk to new people anymore. I introduce my old friends to my new friends with special needs so that we all can meet new people. I have changed my outlook on the people in my classes. The kids with special needs should be in my other classes, too. I have not had the opportunity to be in classes with them before because the teachers shelter us so much that it's as if there is a wall between us. Now that I am taking this communication skills class, the wall is slowly coming down, little by little.

If I had had the chance at an earlier age, I would have taken a class like this. Teachers don't realize that we want to meet kids with disabilities; we're just scared. There are a lot of other kids, too, who would want to take this class, but they don't have the opportunity. It's sad to think that some of the kids with special needs have been going to school with me since elementary school and I never got to know them. A lot of teachers think, "They can't handle this." Well, in fact, we can. We love to do this. Yes, it's hard at first, but we do get to know each other, and it's like magic how we all just work together.

If you could see my class, you would see that all the kids enjoy it. The kids with disabilities learn to listen to us better than to the teachers. I still learn just as much as I would in any other class, it's just taught a bit differently. I wish more of my classes were like this one.

My last advice to everyone is that kids with disabilities are new to inclusion, too, and we are all scared. It might not work out how you planned it in the beginning, but it all comes together. Everyone is the same, no matter if he or she is short, has a broken arm, or needs more help than other kids. We need to treat everyone equally. We all want to know each other; we just need the opportunity.

14

This Is Me

Chad Schrimpf

I don't know why I'm in special education. No one has ever told me the reason. But, I have been in these classes as long as I can remember. School is okay, but I hate it when teachers are mean. I had this one teacher in fifth grade who would make us write 25 sentences every time we talked during class time. I talked a lot, but I couldn't write 25 sentences. The teacher would get mad and yell at me. I would get upset, but it didn't stop me from talking in class.

When I got to sixth grade, they put me in regular ed. classes. The work was way too hard, and the teachers did not try to help me. They went way too fast, and I got confused. I got scared and angry. I needed the help, but none of the teachers seemed to care. They didn't pay attention to me. No one ever noticed that I couldn't keep up with the work they were giving me. They were too busy teaching. They put me back into classes that were out in the portables, away from everyone else. I didn't like being away from all the other kids at school, but at least now I could do the work. I just wish that I could have stayed in the big class where I had made some friends. If nothing else, at least I could have been there as a student aide.

I was so glad when I finally got to high school. This year is different because I'm happier, and I don't really know why. Now, I am 15 years old, and I am a freshman. I have six classes. My favorite subject is art. I love to draw. It calms me down. I can draw anything, but animals are my favorite. I tried to draw a butterfly once, but it turned out like a caterpillar. Sometimes things don't turn out the way I plan. Sometimes the idea I have in my head doesn't come out on paper. But I think my pictures still look good, and drawing things helps me. It's too bad that more teachers don't let me draw in class so I would feel better. I wouldn't be so stressed out and then maybe I could be in more regular ed classes.

Another class I really like is my sixth period. It's called "Peer Buddies." We're working on writing newsletters right now. I'm meeting new people all the time because of this class. Now, meeting new people is easier for me. I met my friend Brittany this year. I went up to her and said, "Hi." We hang out a lot. Heather is also one of my friends. I met her at an art show. She came up to me and introduced me to all of her friends. That was cool.

The rest of my classes are all right. The only class I really don't like is physical education. We're dancing right now. I have no idea what dancing has to do with this class! Physical education should be about sports. Dancing isn't a sport. You don't use sticks or a ball! How can it be a sport? That's the only class really I don't like going to. What makes it worse is that it's my first class of the day.

When I'm not in school, I love to watch movies. I have two whole shelves of videos and DVDs. I like all types of movies especially the ones that make me laugh. I also love computers. I like to surf the Internet and search for sites about cinematography. Cinematography is how movies are made. I wish I could make my own movies. If I could make my own movie it would be sci-fi, something like Star Wars.

I love Star Wars. I have a collection of all the action figures, and I have lots of books about it, too. I read chapter books and picture books if it's about something I like. I read way more at home than I do at school. At home, the books are good. At school, they're boring. I could read all day if it was about something interesting.

The most important thing to know about me is that I'm very sensitive. That's just the way I am. That is my true self. A lot of things hit me hard, and tears pour down my face. That's where my friends help me. They help me a lot. Once, at a school concert in the performing arts center, the music got too loud. Things got out of hand. I was sitting alone at the top of the stairs when Brittany saw that I was upset. She asked me to sit with her. I was glad. The music got to the sensitive part of my heart. It went right through me like an arrow. The sound triggered something in my mind. It was all too much. Tears fell. I had to leave.

My emotions are like a tidal wave. They take over, and I rock back and forth. People tell me to take deep breaths. I only do what they say because I don't want them to get annoyed. But I guess it does help a little bit.

I wouldn't change anything about who I am. Everything about me is good. I am a fun guy because of my sense of humor. I admit it—it can sometimes be annoying, but I think I'm usually pretty funny. My friends say I'm nice and friendly. I wish more people saw that, but no one usually does. I wish my teachers saw it. In fact, my advice to teachers is that you should pay more attention to your students. If you did, you would see that someone like me is a good guy. I'm smart, nice, and funny. I just need some help sometimes.

15

Effective Peer Supports

Susan R. Copeland

On Monday morning, Duane and Jamie were standing outside the door to their high school classroom as students moved through the halls on their way to class. They seemed to be looking for someone as they scanned the dozens of students moving by the doorway. Suddenly, their faces broke into wide grins. Jamie called out, "Hi!" in a loud voice and held up his hand for a high-five from a passing classmate. Duane also spoke, saying, "Guess what I did on Saturday?" Who was this classmate they were so anxiously waiting for? It was Stacey, a junior at the school who had long brown hair pulled back into a ponytail. She and her friends crowded around Duane and Jamie, everyone talking at once as they shared what each had done over the weekend. The second bell rang, and everyone ran for class, including Duane and Jamie.

Although this vignette may seem like a typical interaction between high school students during a passing period, it is actually something new and unusual for these two students. Duane and Jamie are two high school students with extensive support needs attending a large high school in the southeastern part of the country. Jamie rarely speaks unless asked a direct question by someone, and then only in a whisper. Duane is more outgoing but most often communicates with single words and lots of smiles. Before coming to this high school, both young men had received most of their education in segregated, self-contained classrooms. Neither had ever had much contact with their peers without disabilities and certainly had never developed friendships with their general education peers.

Now, both students are attending several general education classes each day. They have met general education peers and developed relationships with them. When they walk through the corridors of their school, they can be seen laughing, smiling, and giving high-fives to other students. They regularly eat lunch with these general education students, something they had never done before.

What made this school experience different from previous ones for Duane, Jamie, and the other students in their special education class? First, their special education teacher worked hard to get both students enrolled in general education classes that met their interests and learning needs. Then, she collaborated with a professor and students from a nearby university to get a peer support program started in her school.

The high school students who became peer buddies (i.e., peer supports) provide academic and social support each day to their classmates with moderate or severe disabilities. This support allows these students to actively participate in general education classes and school activities. Doing so has opened up opportunities to learn new skills and to develop friendships with students they would never have encountered otherwise. Peer supports have allowed these students to become a part of the everyday life of their high schools.

WHAT AND WHO ARE PEER SUPPORTS?

Peer supports are students who, under the guidance of adults such as teachers or administrators, provide various types of direct assistance to their classmates with disabilities (Carter, Hughes, Guth, & Copeland, in press; Copeland et al., 2004). Students acting as peer supports may be enrolled in the same class as the student they are supporting, or they may be students from outside the class who come in to provide support and assistance for a specific class period. Most often, peer supports are students without an identified disability providing assistance to peers with disabilities within inclusive settings, but this is not always the case. Sometimes a student with a learning difference of his or her own may provide assistance and support to another student with a disability (e.g., Brewer, Reid, & Rhine, 2003). For example, Elliott (Chapter 1) and Angela (Chapter 5) were very effective peer supports for some of their high school classmates with disabilities.

What makes peer support programs such as peer buddies or peer tutoring unique is that these models of support allow students to provide academic, behavioral, or social assistance to their peers with disabilities that have traditionally been provided by a classroom teacher or educational assistant. Research has shown that having adults provide the majority of support for students with disabilities can lead to negative consequences for the student being supported. For example, students receiving all of their support from an adult may have fewer opportunities to interact socially with their peers without disabilities; they may become overly dependent on the supporting adult; or their academic progress in a class may be negatively affected (Giangreco, Edelman, Luiselli, & MacFarland, 1997). Angela's story (Chapter 5) illustrates these potential pitfalls clearly. From her perspective, having an adult "hover" constantly was frustrating and socially inhibiting, especially as she grew older.

Peer supports, however, are a more natural form of support. Natural supports are those that are usually present in a given context or setting, are the same or very similar to those used by individuals without disabilities in that context, and are seen as "culturally appropriate" for people in that setting (Luckasson et al., 2002, p. 151). Peer supports meet these conditions. Peers are present in any school setting, so peer support is readily available and doesn't require finding and bringing additional people into a class setting. Students generally provide support for each other in classrooms and school activities, so using peers to assist classmates with disabilities fits in well with typical classroom norms of behavior. For example, who hasn't forgotten to bring a pencil to class and borrowed one from a classmate sitting nearby or asked to see a peer's notes from a missed class? Students acting as peer supports can offer these simple types of assistance, or they can be taught to provide more direct and individualized support for a classmate.

Finally, it is much more usual for students, particularly adolescents, to ask for help from one another than to ask for help from an adult. Peer supports, therefore, may be more "culturally appropriate" than adult support in many school settings. In other words, using peer supports can avoid many of the potentially negative outcomes associated with support from adults while at the same time providing the assistance students with disabilities may need to be successful in general education.

Types of Peer Support Programs

Peer support may be formalized school or systemwide programs that allow participating general education students to earn course credit for acting as peer supports. The Metropolitan-Nashville Peer Buddy

Program is an example of this type of program (Hughes, Guth, Hall, Presley, Dye, & Byers, 1999). The Peer Buddy Program is open to all students in the district's 11 comprehensive high schools. High school students participating in this program enroll in a one-credit elective course and act as peer buddies for their peers with moderate or severe disabilities.

Before beginning the program, students are given a brief orientation on what being a peer support involves; information on disability awareness, communication, and social interaction strategies; and ideas for dealing with inappropriate behavior, should it occur. They also receive a *Peer Buddy Manual* that includes additional information on characteristics of disabilities, disability issues, and strategies for interacting with students with disabilities and handling challenging behavior. Students in the course receive a grade at the end of the semester, just as they do in other classes. Their grade for the Peer Buddy class is based on attendance, teacher observations, and written assignments such as reflection papers or journals.

Peer buddies in the Metropolitan-Nashville Peer Buddy Program provide instructional and noninstructional assistance one class period per day to their peers with disabilities in a variety of school and community settings. Participating general and special education teachers supervise them. The types of support students provide vary and are based on the individual support needs of their peers with disabilities. Most of the peer buddies in this program are junior and senior students, but younger high school students also participate if they have room in their schedules for an elective class. Many of the peer buddies maintain relationships with their peers with disabilities after the Peer Buddy class is completed.

Peer support programs may also be informal arrangements set up by individual classroom teachers in which student volunteers provide assistance and support to their classmates with disabilities or to students with disabilities in other classrooms (Kennedy, 2004; Shukla, Kennedy, & Cushing, 1999). In these arrangements, teachers meet with interested students and provide them with some specific guidance on the type of support their classmate may need. This help might involve assisting students with academic tasks, supporting students' communication, making adaptations to class activities or assignments so that students can actively participate, or providing behavioral support. The supervising adult then frequently monitors the peer support and the student with disabilities to ensure that assistance is provided effectively. What each of these models has in common, however, are peers assisting their classmates instead of adults supporting students.

Support provided by peers can take the form of academic, social, or behavioral assistance. According to Luckasson et al., "Supports have various functions that act to reduce the discrepancy between a person and his or her environmental requirements" (2002, p. 147). Therefore, the type of assistance provided to a classmate with a disability by a peer support can vary widely, depending on the individual needs of the student being supported and the context within which the support occurs. For example, a peer support might take notes for a student with a disability in a history class, invite a classmate with a disability to hang out with his buddies during lunch, provide some informal job coaching for a peer at a school-based worksite, teach a peer to use a self-monitoring strategy to stay on task during classroom activities, assist a peer to shop for clothes at the mall as a part of community-based instruction, or accompany a peer to a school-sponsored club meeting.

It is important to recognize that students may not need the same types or levels of support in every setting and adjust accordingly. Too much support may lead to dependence, and too little may lead to failure. Flexibility and individualization are the keys, and successful programs stress providing just the right amount of support to help a student be successful in a specific context.

Secondary Peer Support Programs

Although a peer support program can be an effective means of providing support at any grade level, these programs are especially useful at the secondary level. As students with disabilities move into secondary schools, they are more likely to be placed in separate classroom settings that offer few opportunities to interact with general education peers (U.S. Department of Education, 2002). Also, unlike elementary school, at the secondary level students change classes frequently during the school day. This means that students with disabilities who are enrolled in general education classes may be with different students and teachers every period, which may make it more difficult to establish social relationships. Frequent class changes also mean that students must learn the expectations of several teachers in different curricular areas. Keeping the requirements for each class straight can seem overwhelming to some students, and they will need assistance and support to be successful.

Secondary teachers themselves face a multitude of challenges that may affect their ability to support students with disabilities, including large class sizes, pressure to prepare students for high-stakes tests, and limited time to plan and collaborate with special educators or related-services personnel (Tralli, Colombo, & Deshler, 1996). These factors may make it difficult for teachers to plan and implement the individualized supports students with disabilities need to be successful in gaining access to the general curriculum. Utilization of peer supports is one effective way to offer the supports secondary students with disabilities may need to benefit from participating in general education.

BENEFITS OF A PEER SUPPORT PROGRAM

Participating in peer support programs has numerous benefits for students with and without disabilities. Teachers who have peer supports in their classrooms also experience positive outcomes. One of the most important benefits of a peer support program is that it can increase access to the general curriculum for students with disabilities. Legislation (e.g., No Child Left Behind, 2001 [PL 107-110]; the Individuals with Disabilities Education Act Amendments of 1997 [PL 105-17]) has mandated that all students have access to the same challenging curriculum and that they be provided with the supports needed to make progress in this curriculum. This shift in provision of special education services from separate, segregated settings to inclusive settings has challenged educators to facilitate meaningful participation in general education for *all* students. Simply being present in an inclusive environment is not sufficient for students to experience academic and social success. Students with disabilities often need modifications, accommodations, and assistance to maximize their experiences in general education. Following are some specific ways in which peer supports can benefit participating students.

Academic Benefits

One of the most common ways peer supports assist their classmates with disabilities is in providing tutoring or extra assistance in academic skills. High school general education teachers have reported that peer supports provide needed opportunities for individualized instruction for their peers with disabilities that may be difficult for teachers to implement given large class sizes (Copeland, McCall, et al., 2002). Some examples of this type of support provided by peers might be providing one-to-one tutoring on a particular academic skill (e.g., writing a three-point essay), studying together for a test, taking notes for a classmate during a teacher lecture and then explaining the key concepts from the lecture, reading a test to a classmate and recording the answers, or assisting a peer to participate in a cooperative learning project.

Secondary general educators participating in the Metropolitan-Nashville Peer Buddy Program reported that academic peer support for students with disabilities was more successful when the student providing the support was actually enrolled in the same class as the student receiving supports or when the peer support had previously taken the class (Copeland, McCall, et al., 2002). These teachers found that students with some background knowledge about the information and skills taught in the course could more easily modify or explain class assignments or activities than students without this experience.

The peer buddies that we interviewed pointed out that not all teachers in their high schools had high expectations for students with disabilities or believed that these students could acquire class content and skills (Copeland et al., 2004). The peer buddies also observed that not all teachers they encountered provided the individualized assistance some students need to make academic progress in a class. These peer buddies saw the support they gave their partners (peers with disabilities) in general education classes as critical to ensuring that the partners had access to the general curriculum and were successful.

Using peer supports to provide academic assistance may also be more acceptable to students with disabilities than having that support provided by an adult (a teacher or educational assistant). Few adolescents want to spend the majority of their time at school hanging out with adults! Some participants in the Metropolitan-Nashville Peer Buddy Program, for example, reported that they preferred having a classmate instead of an adult provide any extra help they might need in their general education classes. They perceived that using peer supports made them less likely to appear different from their peers. This is an important consideration when working with any adolescent because they may be less likely to ask for assistance if they believe doing so will be stigmatizing and thus may miss out on the assistance they need to be successful in their general education classes.

Social Benefits

It is now recognized that access to the general curriculum involves not only opportunities to participate in a challenging academic curriculum but also opportunities to gain access to the other myriad

social and extracurricular activities that make up the school experience (Hughes, Rung, Wehmeyer, Agran, Copeland, & Hwang, 2000;
Ryndak & Billingsley, 2004). These additional components of the
general curriculum allow students to explore new interests and provide occasions to develop and utilize valued academic and social
skills. Developing social competence, for example, is a critical skill
for all students, leading to development of friendships and improved
quality of life.

Social competence is developed by repeated interactions with
others (i.e., peers; Kennedy, Cushing, & Itkonen, 1997). If students
are only allowed to interact with others with disabilities, it is
unlikely they will observe and learn typical social interaction behaviors leading to social competence (Kennedy, 2001). For students with
disabilities, social interaction with peers without disabilities is also
associated with additional positive outcomes that include development of academic, functional, and leisure skills (Hughes et al., 2001).
Therefore, opportunities for social interaction are important for the
development and well-being of students.

Sadly, though, even when high school students are placed in
inclusive settings, relatively little social interaction may take place
between students with and without disabilities (e.g., Mu, Siegel, &
Allinder, 2000). Students with disabilities may miss out on opportunities to interact with general education classmates unless teachers
or other adults structure and prompt social interaction between these
students (Hughes, Carter, Bradford, & Copeland, 2002). Research has
shown, however, that interaction between these groups of students
does increase when peer supports are in place. Carter et al. (in press),
for example, found that the quality and frequency of social interaction between high school students with severe disabilities and their
general education classmates increased when peer buddies were present in the setting. In fact, having these peer supports present was
more closely associated with increased social interaction than even
the level of integration of the setting itself. In other words, even
when students with disabilities are in inclusive environments with
their general education peers, they are not as likely to interact unless
peer buddies are there to support the interaction.

Peer supports, then, are a natural, unobtrusive way to enhance
and facilitate social interaction between students with disabilities
and their peers. When we asked high school peer buddies how they
thought they helped their partners (classmates with disabilities),
61% of them said they did so by being a friend to their partner or
helping their partner to learn how to make friends (Hughes et al.,
2001). Other peer buddies discussed the importance of helping their

partners feel a part of the school's academic and social activities (Copeland et al., 2004). Clearly, these students recognized the value placed on social relationships by adolescents and felt that one of the most important benefits of the peer support program was helping their classmates with disabilities develop and experience new relationships.

So, how do peer supports provide social support to their classmates with disabilities? Social support may be as simple as the peer support introducing a classmate to his or her friends, thus increasing the social network of the student with disabilities. Meeting more people can naturally lead to increased interactions with peers and opportunities to develop friendships. In fact, when talking with peer buddies participating in the Metropolitan-Nashville Peer Buddy Program, we found that many of them were "recruited" by their friends who had been peer buddies. They had met classmates with disabilities through their friends taking the peer buddy course and gotten to be friends with these classmates. These interactions caused them to sign up to be a peer support so they could spend more time with their new friends. These peer buddies also listed things such as inviting a classmate with a disability to eat lunch with them and their friends, talking in the hall during passing periods, attending a school basketball game together, or inviting a peer to join them and their friends in renting a limousine to attend the high school prom as examples of the social support they provided.

Another form of social support includes interacting with a peer during a leisure activity and modeling appropriate social behaviors and interaction styles. This support can be particularly important for students who have spent most of their time at school in self-contained classes and have had little opportunity to see interaction patterns typical of their peers without disabilities. Sometimes, social support involves teaching a specific social skill to a student. Peer buddies in one school, for example, taught their partners to use communication books to initiate conversations with other general education peers, leading to increased interaction between students with and without disabilities and the development of new friendships (Hughes et al., 2000).

Social relationships are an important source of support for everyone (Kennedy, 2004). Teachers and peer buddies have reported over and over that participating in a peer support program has led to development of close relationships between the peer support and his or her classmate with disabilities (Copeland, McCall, et al., 2002). As one peer buddy put it, "Most of all I've helped by being a true friend" (Hughes et al., 2001, p. 350). Establishing relationships with others can lead to feelings of acceptance and community, things that are important to everyone.

Reciprocal Nature of Peer Supports

Students who take on the role of a peer support also benefit from their participation in these programs. Peer support programs truly are a two-way street! Students with disabilities receive benefits, but students providing the support also gain valuable skills and experiences. Peer buddies we questioned, for example, spoke of experiencing personal growth, making new friends, increasing their knowledge about disabilities, and improving their interpersonal skills (Hughes et al., 2001).

They also reported that being a peer support was fun! This theme was repeated over and over. Students enjoyed the time they spent providing support and wanted other students in their high schools to hear about the program and sign up.

General education teachers supervising peer supports in the Metropolitan-Nashville Peer Buddy Program observed that participating students increased their understanding of diversity and disability and showed an increased awareness of social issues and sense of civic responsibility (Copeland, McCall, et al., 2002). One administrator mentioned that serving as a peer support could be beneficial to all students, not just the "best" students. He believed that being a peer support provided some of the seniors at his school a reason to stay in school (Copeland, Hughes, & Carter, 2002). Another administrator discussed the development of leadership skills that he saw in the peer supports and the opportunity this program provided for service learning. Teachers also commented that they felt the students with disabilities were often positive role models for the students without disabilities. By demonstrating a real interest in class topics, for example, and working hard to complete assignments, students with disabilities modeled effective classroom behavior for their peers without disabilities.

When asked about their perceptions of personal benefits from participating in peer support programs, peer buddies we talked with also mentioned that even general education students not participating in the peer support program receive benefits from the program (Copeland et al., 2004). These peer buddies noticed that peer support programs increased the academic and social participation of students with disabilities in all aspects of high school life in their schools. They commented that this increased participation offered new opportunities for general education students to meet and interact with classmates they had never before had the chance to meet. These interactions then lead to the development of new friendships and increased all students' awareness of disability issues.

Benefits for Teachers

Peer support programs benefit more than just the students involved. Classroom general and special education teachers also experience positive outcomes. Teachers and peer buddies we spoke with mentioned several benefits for teachers including assistance in providing individualized instruction for students with disabilities, reduced time that teachers must spend in providing one-to-one instruction, increased professional growth (e.g., knowing that they are teaching *all* students), and increased personal satisfaction of watching students working together so that everyone was learning (Copeland, McCall, et al., 2002; Copeland et al., 2004).

SETTING UP EFFECTIVE PEER SUPPORTS

As mentioned previously, peer support programs may be formalized, credit-bearing courses, or they can be informal arrangements created by a classroom teacher and student volunteers. Regardless of the model selected, there are some important things to keep in mind when planning to implement peer supports. Following are some suggestions for facilitating an effective peer support program taken from interviews with peer buddies, teachers, and administrators (Copeland, McCall, et al., 2002; Copeland et al., 2004; Hughes et al., 1999).

First, actively recruit students to be peer supports. Don't assume that students will know about these opportunities and volunteer on their own. Our experience with the Metropolitan-Nashville Peer Buddy Program suggests that students are less likely to read formal school announcements about new school activities and courses and are more likely to hear about such programs from their friends. Be sure that all school personnel are aware of the peer support program, and encourage faculty and staff to send students to you that they believe would be a good match for the program.

Don't forget to recruit both male and female students. "Helper" roles are often associated with being female; however, male students can provide positive role models for their peers and are just as likely to experience benefits from being a peer support as their female classmates. Peer support programs are good for everyone!

Next, screen students wishing to be peer supports. This process can take the form of an interview or a formal application, but it should provide sufficient information to determine if the student has the interests and skills needed to support classmates with disabilities (Brewer et al., 2003; Copeland, McCall, et al., 2002). Remember that you aren't looking for the "best" students, but for those with a genuine interest in supporting classmates.

Our research has shown that one adult typically has served as the key person in promoting a peer support program in a school. Although this seems to be an effective way to get started, it is also important to increase participation in and ownership of the program if it is to sustain itself. Let everyone—teachers, educational assistants, administrators, secretaries, guidance counselors, parents— know about the program and about the benefits for general and special education students and teachers who participate. This may mean providing school in-services, speaking at a Parent Teacher Association event, or offering opportunities for individuals to visit classrooms where peer supports are in place. Many faculty and staff are not aware of the potential benefits from such programs. They will become strong supporters once they realize the benefits that these programs can provide to their school.

One highly effective way to advertise a peer support program is to create a newsletter that includes ideas, activities, and stories related to successful peer supports in your school or district. It can include strategies teachers and students have used to increase academic or social support in classes or school activities, ideas for recruiting peer supports, or personal stories about participating in a peer support program. The peer supports themselves, as well as the students being supported, teachers, administrators, and parents can contribute their ideas and creative suggestions.

Even if you decide to use an informal peer support model, establish clear expectations of the support role students are to fill, and explain these expectations to students before they begin offering support to classmates. Teachers and peer buddies in our studies stressed the importance of clear communication between all parties before students begin to assist classmates.

Another recommendation from peer buddies is for teachers to initially structure activities for interaction between the peer support and the student receiving support. Peer buddies felt that this point was especially important if the student receiving support has more extensive support needs and if the two students don't know each other well. In the past, the majority of students with moderate or severe disabilities have received their education in self-contained classrooms. This meant that general education students had few opportunities to interact with them. It is probably unreasonable to expect students to immediately feel comfortable and competent interacting with classmates with extensive support needs without being provided some structure and support of their own. Structured activities help break the ice and get the relationship off to a great start.

Monitoring interactions between the peer support and his or her partner frequently is also important. Be sure the peer support has regular opportunities to talk with the supervising adult to ask questions or discuss his or her experiences. Students can learn to provide fairly intensive levels of support, but they need guidance and assistance from you to do so successfully. Peer buddies with whom we worked emphasized the importance of having general sources of information about disability and instructional support, such as the *Peer Buddy Manual,* available. They also believed that it was important to give peer supports specific information on communication and behavioral support strategies for their partners.

Keep in mind that peer supports are *not* educational assistants. Be clear about the goals of your peer support program. Develop support roles for participating students that meet these goals, and be explicit in communicating these goals to administrators, teachers, and participating students.

In addition, talk regularly with students receiving support to see how the support relationships are going from their perspective. Sometimes, adjustments may need to be made in who is providing support or in the level or type of support provided. Supervising adults may not be aware of difficulties unless they take the time to ask students about their perceptions.

Be sure that students with disabilities are involved in the same activities in classes and other settings as their general education peers. Teach peer supports to provide assistance and modifications in ways that don't call undue attention to the student receiving supports.

Finally, strive for natural proportions of students with and without disabilities in general education classrooms. It will ensure that all students receive the level of supports they require in a manner that doesn't create unwanted attention.

SUMMARY

Peer support is a valuable method of assisting *all* students to gain access to the academic and social life of their school communities.

Peer support programs have been unanimously endorsed by administrators, special and general educators, parents, and students with and without disabilities because everyone who participates benefits. As educators, we must continue to develop models of schooling that meet the diverse abilities, backgrounds, and interests of today's students. Peer support is a valuable tool for creating schools that are truly inclusive.

REFERENCES

Brewer, R.D., Reid, M.S., & Rhine, B.G. (2003). Peer coaching: Students teaching to learn. *Intervention in School and Clinic, 39*(2), 113–126.

Carter, E.W., Hughes, C., Guth, C., & Copeland, S.R. (in press). Factors influencing social interaction among high school students with intellectual disabilities and their general education peers. *American Journal on Mental Retardation.*

Copeland, S.R., Hughes, C., & Carter, E.W. (2002). *Multiple perspectives of a high school peer support program: What do students, teachers, and parents say?* Paper presented at the annual meeting of TASH, Boston.

Copeland, S.R., Hughes, C., Carter, E.W., Guth, C., Presley, J.A., Williams, C.R., & Fowler, S.E. (2004). Increasing access to general education: Perspectives of participants in a high school peer support program. *Remedial and Special Education, 26*, 342–352.

Copeland, S.R., McCall, J., Williams, C.R., Guth, C., Carter, E.W., Fowler, S.E., Presley, J.A., & Hughes, C. (2002). High school peer buddies: A win-win situation. *TEACHING Exceptional Children, 35*(1), 16–21.

Giangreco, M.F., Edelman, S.W., Luiselli, T.E., & MacFarland, S.C. (1997). Helping or hovering? Effects of instructional assistant proximity on students with disabilities. *Exceptional Children, 64*, 7–18.

Hughes, C., Carter, E.W., Bradford, E., & Copeland, S.R. (2002). Effects of instructional versus non-instructional roles on the social interactions of high school students. *Education and Training in Mental Retardation and Developmental Disabilities, 37*, 146–162.

Hughes, C., Copeland, S.R., Guth, C., Rung, L.L., Hwang, B., Kleeb, G., & Strong, M. (2001). General education students' perspectives on their involvement in a high school peer buddy program. *Education and Training in Mental Retardation and Developmental Disabilities, 36*, 343–356.

Hughes, C., Guth, C., Hall, S., Presley, J., Dye, M., & Byers, C. (1999). "They are my best friends": Peer buddies promote inclusion in high school. *TEACHING Exceptional Children, 31*, 32–37.

Hughes, C., Rung, L.L., Wehmeyer, M.L., Agran, M., Copeland, S.R., & Hwang, B. (2000). Self-prompted communication book use to increase social interaction among high school students. *Journal of The Association for Persons with Severe Disabilities, 25*, 153–166.

Individuals with Disabilities Education Act Amendments of 1997, PL 105-17, 20 U.S.C. §§ 1400 *et seq.*

Kennedy, C.H. (2001). Social interaction interventions for youth with severe disabilities should emphasize interdependence. *Mental Retardation and Developmental Disabilities Research Reviews, 7,* 122–127.

Kennedy, C.H. (2004). Social relationships. In C.H. Kennedy & E.M. Horn (Eds.), *Including students with severe disabilities* (pp. 100–119). Boston: Allyn & Bacon.

Kennedy, C.H., Cushing, L.S., & Itkonen, T. (1997). General education participation improves the social contacts and friendship networks of students with severe disabilities. *Journal of Behavioral Education, 7,* 167–189.

Luckasson, R., Borthwick-Duffy, S., Buntinx, W.H.E., Coulter, D.L., Craig, E.M., Reeve, A., Schalock, R.L., Snell, M.E., Spitalinik, D.M., Spreat, S., & Tasse, M.J. (2002). *Mental retardation: Definition, classification, and systems of support* (10th ed.). Washington, DC: American Association on Mental Retardation.

Mu, K., Siegel, E.B., & Allinder, R.M. (2000). Peer interactions and sociometric status of high school students with moderate or severe disabilities in general education classrooms. *Journal of The Association for Persons with Severe Handicaps, 25,* 142–152.

No Child Left Behind Act of 2001, PL 107-110, 20 U.S.C. §§ 6301 *et seq.*

Ryndak, D.L., & Billingsley, F. (2004). Access to the general education curriculum. In C. Kennedy & E.M. Horn (Eds.), *Including students with severe disabilities.* Boston: Allyn & Bacon.

Shukla, S., Kennedy, C.H., & Cushing, L.S. (1999). Intermediate school students with severe disabilities: Supporting their social participation in general education classrooms. *Journal of Positive Behavior Interventions, 1,* 130–140.

Tralli, R., Colombo, B., & Deshler, D.D. (1996). The strategies intervention model: A model for supported inclusion at the secondary level. *Remedial and Special Education, 17,* 204–216.

U.S. Department of Education. (2002). *Twenty-fourth annual report to Congress on the implementation of the Individuals with Disabilities Education Act.* Washington, DC: Author.

16

Connecting Across the Community

Pen Pals in Inclusive Classrooms

Veronica M. Moore, Carolyn Metzler, and Stacey Pearson

"Pen pals are real fun to have because it's like you have an older brother or sister. You can send messages back and forth."
—a second grade student

Teachers are always looking for new and innovative ways to improve their practice. Although there are varied approaches to enhance writing skills, we chose to create an innovative program that improves literacy across grade levels while promoting inclusion, acceptance, and diversity. We refer to this as our pen pal program. Over the course of the school year, this writing project blossomed into a wonderful collaborative partnership between elementary and high school students and teachers. We would like to share the origins of our program, the four components of the program, and a summary of what we learned from the process.

HOW WE GOT STARTED

We all taught in inclusive settings but in different schools. Carolyn and Stacey were team teaching a second-grade inclusive class in which Veronica's daughter was a student. Veronica was coteaching an inclusive communication skills class at the high school down the street. When we first met at registration, we realized that we were all educators who philosophically agreed on the importance of inclusion. A sense of camaraderie developed among us as we realized that even though we taught different grade levels, our approaches and views about teaching children were surprisingly similar.

Early in the school year, we were comparing notes about our goals for our classes, the standards we had to meet, and the ways we were planning to implement literacy instruction in our respective inclusive settings. Preparing writing lessons for diverse classes is always a difficult task. Often, the process can be dull, and we were discussing options on how to make it more exciting for the students and for us. Then, we had an idea. What about pen pals? It is not uncommon for classes to correspond with students from other countries—why not do it with the students down the street?

Letter writing was part of the required high school communication skills curriculum. It was also a component of the state-mandated standards for elementary school students. We became energized about this new project and immediately went to work to make this an enjoyable and meaningful experience for the students. The initial steps took extensive planning. Also, we learned substantially more from our successes and our mistakes.

FOUR COMPONENTS OF AN INCLUSIVE PEN PAL PROGRAM

This section outlines the four major components that we suggest other teachers consider when setting up similar programs in their own schools.

Communication and Collaboration

Before teachers embark on any project, it is important that they share similar philosophical views about students. Even though teachers may see each other only sporadically throughout the school year, it is crucial that they consider themselves to be a team. To accomplish this, teachers should communicate regularly through meetings, e-mail, or telephone conversations. As with all teaming situations, teachers need to communicate with each other about their expectations. Admittedly, collaborating with a colleague, especially one who is not at your school site, can initially be a difficult task. We have found that the collaborative planning form provided by Keefe, Moore, and Duff (2004) to be a useful tool to begin the dialogue between colleagues.

Before the students begin writing to each other, teachers should discuss logistics such as the frequency of the letter exchanges; appropriate pairing of students based on interests, personalities, and writing abilities; potential field trips; and community service activities. It is important to discuss the needs and strengths of each student and to pair each student with a partner who is compatible.

Diversity and Acceptance

When implementing an inclusive pen pal program, teachers should remind their classes about individual differences. Educating students about diversity in advance is important because some of the students may have significant, visible needs or use alternate forms of communication. The method in which teachers approach the issue can vary. For example, one teacher may initiate a discussion on the importance of differences and acceptance. Another may read a children's book that focuses on the same subject. Whatever technique a teacher chooses to address the issues of diversity, it is important that he or she actively involves students in the discussion and solicits their questions and advice. Many times, students find easy solutions to situations that adults perceive to be challenging.

We have seen disabilities become invisible and relationships develop between pen pals based on personalities and interests. Of the many times we have witnessed this occurrence, one of the most memorable was the relationship that transpired between Lauren and Joey. Lauren had cerebral palsy and was nonverbal. She corresponded with Joey, her elementary school pen pal, by using a specially equipped computer. Communication through the letter exchanges went smoothly due to the use of assistive technology; however, the classes were going to meet, and we were concerned about how Lauren and Joey were going to communicate without a computer. Lauren entered the room, and we watched anxiously as the two met for the first time. We waited to see Joey's reaction and were ready to jump in and offer assistance. None was needed.

Lauren and Joey bonded immediately. Joey quickly figured out on his own that Lauren could answer "yes" and "no" questions. He remembered her interests from her letters, and he drew her pictures of her favorite cartoon characters. The meeting was a success. Joey was not concerned with the fact that his pen pal had significant disabilities. He just saw a girl who liked SpongeBob. Joey commented later that "Lauren was really fun to hang out with because she liked SpongeBob, and she had a cool Christmas tree on her wheelchair."

When teachers educate students about diversity and create a welcoming classroom that embraces and accepts differences, the students, themselves, figure out ways to make everyone feel welcome.

Writing the Letters

As with any instructional activity, the way one introduces it to the students greatly affects its success. When teachers begin the writing process, they should discuss rules and expectations with students and include the students in creating ground rules regarding the content of the letters. Sometimes, the high school students need gentle reminders about the use of "slang" in their writing and topics that are appropriate for elementary school students. Teachers should allow the older students to step back in time and reminisce about their favorite elementary school memories. As one sophomore recalled, "My pen pal liked Ninja Turtles. Those were my favorites when I was a kid. I didn't even know they were still around. This brought back great memories."

Teachers should let the older students initiate the letter writing so that the elementary school students have a model to follow. For instance, the high school students could begin by introducing themselves and writing about their interests (e.g., sports, characters, books, movies, school activities) or hobbies. They can also create questions for the elementary students to answer. Figure 16.1 shows a high school student's letter.

Sometimes, the younger children have difficulties beginning the writing process. Composing letters is a difficult skill for many children, and teachers should use a variety of prompts for students who struggle with the process. Prompts may include teacher-generated questions, acronym poetry, or simple brainstorming sessions. A copy of an elementary school student's letter is shown in Figure 16.2.

Although corresponding with someone outside of the classroom is an enjoyable activity, there are ways that the pen pal project can be enhanced. Sending pictures to each other is a useful way to make this experience come alive. The students enjoy seeing pictures of their pen pals, and it helps them make the connection that their letters will be read by an actual person. Another method to enhance the project is by allowing students to incorporate various craft ideas in the letter. Popsicle sticks, glitter, glue, gel pens, paint pens, construction paper, and markers make the letters more personal and alleviate some of the stress associated with writing. There are many creative ways to present the letter, and the students seem to

Figure 16.1.   Pen pal letter written by a high school student.

enjoy finding find new and more elaborate ways to make their letters interesting.

As one elementary school student mentioned, "I like writing the letters because it's detailed. You get to design the cards and letters any way you want." A high school student shared the same sentiment, "I haven't used glue or markers in ages. I forgot how much fun this is." Both sets of students really took pleasure in writing the letters.

Opportunities to Meet

Although the students enjoy writing back and forth, this activity is not enough. Students need proximity to each other and awareness of each other's physical being. They need to form some type of personal contact to tie the experience together. Therefore, it is important for the group to meet. This could be a seasonal party, card/gift exchange, or get together at a park for snacks and games.

When our group got together, the younger students saw the older ones as role models, regardless of whether the high school students had disabilities that may have been apparent to others. There were no schisms between the "regular" and the "special" kids. Everyone played together on the playground or on the field. The teenagers relished the opportunities to act like little kids again. They played on the swings, tossed water balloons, smacked the tetherball, and rolled in the grass. The elementary school students were elated when the high school students entered their world. One student said, "They were fun. They like to do the things I like to do."

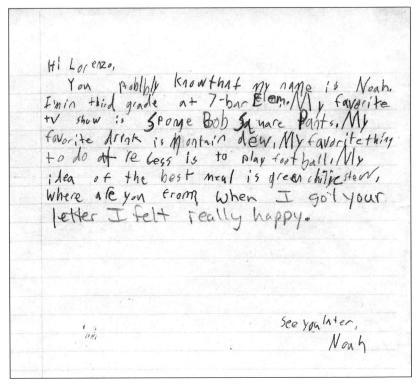

Figure 16.2.   Pen pal letter written by an elementary school student.

The students cared enough about each other to make sure everyone was included in the activities. This concern was apparent when we gathered for a game of Red Rover at the park. During the game, high school students in wheelchairs were pushed by their elementary pen pals so that they were not excluded from the fun.

One young man with disabilities was overwhelmed by the exuberance of the students and opted to sit out and merely watch from the sidelines. His elementary school pen pal noticed his anxiety. She approached us and said, "He looks sad. Can I hang out with him on the monkey bars?" She assumed the responsibility of making sure her pen pal felt welcomed and accepted. We, as teachers, gave him permission not to participate without considering his feelings. His pen pal sensed his loneliness right away and took steps to alleviate it.

WHAT WE LEARNED

The outcomes of this pen pal program were more than we anticipated. We saw an increased motivation and improvement in writing across curricular areas. We also witnessed various friendships develop among the students. We saw that exposing students to diverse populations led to widespread acceptance and tolerance. Overwhelmingly, the elementary school children who had pen pals with significant disabilities only saw the person, not the disability.

Setting up an inclusive pen pal program requires careful coordination and collaboration between the teachers; however, that is just one step in the process. Our program was successful because it was student led. We created appropriate matches between pen pals and facilitated the writing process, but the students decided the content of their letters and the types of activities that ensued. Programs like ours not only increase literacy skills but they also provide avenues for children to experience diversity.

REFERENCES

Keefe, E.B., Moore, V., & Duff, F. (2004). The four knows of collaborative teaching. *TEACHING Exceptional Children, 36*(5), 36–42.

III

School Implementation

17

This Is Their School

Stanley Agustin and Elizabeth B. Keefe

I walked into the middle school on a very cold morning. As I approached the door, it swung open, and a young man held the door open for me. I smiled and thanked him. He smiled, too. Inside, students were milling around, but I didn't see any adults. I immediately wondered if I should "do something." What was going on here? My own experience in schools was that students were not allowed in the building until after the first bell. School wasn't scheduled to start for at least 20 more minutes, so I knew the bell had not rung. When I commented to Stan (the principal) on my surprise, he looked at me and smiled, "Liz, this is their school. Why shouldn't they be inside?"

This is their school. These four words may not seem like much, but they say everything about the vision and focus of Memories Middle School (MMS). MMS is a school where students come first, where systems change has been embraced over many years to implement democratic schooling and least restrictive environment. It is a school committed to student-centered learning, where students feel they belong and have a voice in their education.

MMS has an enrollment of 910 students. The student population is 82% Hispanic, 14% Anglo American, 2% African American, 1% Native American, and 1% other. The school is located in an area of low socioeconomic status shown by the free and reduced lunch rate of 75%. The special education population is 22%. Stanley "Stan" Agustin has been at this school for a total of 17 years—3 years as a teacher, 8 years as the assistant principal, and 6 years as the principal.

Elizabeth "Liz" B. Keefe is an Associate Professor at the University of New Mexico who spends at least 1 day per week at MMS and is proud to be considered an unofficial staff member.

THE CIRCLE OF COURAGE AS A FRAMEWORK

"Belonging, mastery, independence, and generosity are universal human needs. In a society that believes all children are sacred beings, these become the birthrights of all of our children."
—Brendtro, Brokenleg, and Van Bockern (1990, p. 138)

We would like to share the story of MMS within the context of the Circle of Courage (Brendtro et al., 1990). The principles of the Circle of Courage have guided the systemic reform efforts at MMS as the school has embraced the vision of improving the social and educational outcomes of all students through democratic and inclusive education. The Circle of Courage conceptualizes a strengths-based approach to child development and education. This holistic approach to education acknowledges that "Fostering self-esteem is a primary goal in socializing all children" (Brendtro et al., 1990, p. 44).

When Europeans invaded North America, they viewed native people as less developed, but according to Brendtro et al., "Native peoples possessed profound child psychology wisdom that might well have been adopted by the immigrants to North America" (1990, p. 44). Brendtro et al. believed that four values of traditional native approaches to childrearing—belonging, mastery, independence, and generosity—provide a positive culture for education. Lakota Sioux artist George Blue Bird portrayed these values within a medicine wheel (see Van Bockern, Brendtro, & Brokenleg, 2000, p. 62).

SPIRIT OF BELONGING

Brendtro et al. stated, "In traditional Native society, it was the duty of all adults to serve as teachers for younger persons" (1990, p. 46). This practice fosters a strong sense of community and belonging across generations. Schools form a significant part of children's environment, so it is critical that children feel a sense of community and belonging in school. The importance of belonging is also stressed by Kunc, who stated, "Maslow . . . pointed out that belonging is an essential and prerequisite human need that must be met before an individual can achieve a sense of self-worth" (2000, p. 80).

The sense of community and belonging is palpable at MMS today, but it was not always this way. As recently as the early 1990s, the school was divided physically. General education classes were located in the main buildings, and all special education programs were housed in portable classrooms. In the mid 1990s, special education programs were finally placed next to regular education classes. At the end of the 1990s, the sixth grade academy decided to pilot a team-taught inclusive classroom after seeing a presentation by a team from another school. Success stories abounded from the inclusive class. Not only were students with disabilities more successful, but general education staff also noted how great it was to have another adult in the class who worked with all students. The result was that all students' needs were met more effectively.

After the success of the sixth grade academy, the seventh and eighth grade academies implemented inclusive programs the next year. The successes of all of the students in these classrooms continued to fuel and confirm the importance of educating students with disabilities in general education. The teachers observed that the students demonstrated a rise in self-confidence and self-esteem, an increase in socialization skills, and ultimately an increase in academic skills as well. Staff members determined that inclusive education should absolutely continue.

Although some of MMS's students with disabilities were educated in team-taught classrooms, the majority were served in a segregated environment for most of the day. Through collaboration between MMS and the University of New Mexico, and with support from the New Mexico Public Education Department, all students with disabilities at MMS were provided the opportunity to be educated in general education for most of the day. Inclusive education was implemented through a variety of support systems including team teaching and consult models.

The move to educating students with disabilities in general education settings made a big difference for the students. They experienced dramatic positive social and academic changes. We believe that many of these changes are due to the fact that students with disabilities are no longer in portables. They finally belong to the school community.

One teacher surveyed his students about the change from being in small classes to being in larger classes. The students were overwhelmingly positive and mentioned over and over that they had more friends in the larger classes. Parents are also very happy with the changes and have told the school administration and teachers that being in general education classrooms has improved their children's achievement, self-esteem, and attitude toward school.

The students with disabilities at MMS were thrilled to be included in general education classes. Although the students' individualized education programs (IEPs) the year before had indicated that that they would be placed in general education, some students who received special education services still did not realize what was going to happen until they found themselves in general education classes. At the beginning of the school year, several students motioned to Stan and quietly asked, "Mr. Agustin, did they make a mistake with my schedule?" The reply was, "No." Then, they said, "Please Mr. Agustin, don't change my schedule to what it was last year." This statement was a strong indication that we had made the right decision.

The spirit of belonging at MMS goes beyond the classroom. As described at the start of this chapter, this school belongs to the students and the community. Parents are an important part of the school and are welcomed as partners. Their importance is made clear in numerous ways, including the school's parent office. Parents are also invited to be part of the leadership, and regular parent meetings ensure that parents are consulted and informed about school issues and initiatives. MMS is a school where all people are made to feel instantly welcome by students and staff.

SPIRIT OF MASTERY

The value of mastery in schools is one that is front and center in the current accountability climate created by federal and state legislation. Unfortunately, mastery is primarily measured in a very limited way through testing in the areas of reading, writing, and math. In contrast, Brendtro et al. noted, "The simple wisdom of Native culture was that since all need to feel competent, all must be encouraged in their competency" (1990, p. 51). Through achieving competence, students will experience success and be motivated to continue to achieve.

One example of the way in which MMS has restructured to improve educational and social outcomes for students has been the implementation of the academy concept. This approach provides smaller learning communities within the larger school environment. MMS has gone through a systemic change of its organizational structure. Through this process, the traditional system of top-down administration has been transformed into a democratic, collaborative leadership team that includes the parent community.

The grade-level academies support the concept of smaller learning. Each academy meets once a week to discuss instructional issues and student concerns. Proactive parent conferences for academic, behavior, and/or truancy concerns are the responsibilities of each academy community. Every member has an equal voice, and decisions are reached through consensus.

The grade-level academies have provided a personalized approach to education. Because of this empowerment and ownership, there has been a dramatic shift in how teachers work with students. An example of this shift is that when one teaching approach does not work for a student, teachers place the emphasis on finding other strategies rather than blaming the student.

The change in organizational structure, together with the increased diversity of students in classrooms, has led to the implementation of student-centered instructional strategies such as cooperative learning (Johnson, Johnson, & Holubec, 1993), differentiated instruction (Tomlinson, 2001), and multiple intelligences (Armstrong, 2001). In addition, schoolwide approaches to literacy have been adopted and implemented with the support of targeted professional development by local and national experts. The use of these instructional strategies has improved academic achievement for all students.

SPIRIT OF INDEPENDENCE

The Spirit of Independence is characterized by Brendtro et al. as follows, "Free will is cultivated by responsibility so that the child can say 'I have the power to make decisions' " (1990, p. 138). Children will not be able to make good choices if they do not have the opportunity to make decisions. Native people did not believe in approaches to discipline that emphasize rewards and punishment. Rather, "Native elders believed that if children are to be taught responsibility, they must be approached with maturity and dignity" (Brendtro et al., 1990, p. 53). The value of independence has particular implications for how schools approach issues around students' behavior and discipline.

In the early 1990s, MMS was a school in crisis because the staff had become reactive rather than proactive due to the gang activities, drugs, and weapons. Student conflicts were a routine part of our school day. The staff's time was spent constantly putting out fires. Behavior concerns in the classrooms were a major problem. Six years ago, the administrative team received more than 1,500 behavior referrals for the first semester alone. Something had to be done because the traditional approach of reprimanding these students clearly wasn't working!

As a result, MMS staff decided to implement a schoolwide positive behavior support program centered on the use of an accountability card for each student (see Figure 17.1). Each classroom has a Code of Conduct collaboratively developed by the students and teachers. The accountability card helps teachers and students clearly understand the expectations for behavior in the classroom. It becomes a tool for providing guidance to the students so they can make choices with regard to their behavior.

The student and teacher share responsibility for keeping the accountability card completed each day. This card allows teachers and students to comment or check off a continuum of potential behavior issues and document positive behaviors for each class period. Staff, parents, and students all had input into the development and implementation of the accountability card system. After the introduction of the accountability card stragegy, the referrals to the office for behavior immediately reduced to an average of one per week, which resulted in more time for the administrators to function as educational leaders and more time for teachers to focus on instructional priorities in the classroom.

SPIRIT OF GENEROSITY

Brendtro et al. (1990) reported that the principle of generosity is one of the most highly valued characteristics of native people. "Giving was not confined to property but rather permeated all aspects of Native American culture" (1990, p. 58). Van Bockern et al. suggested that many schools do not foster the spirit of generosity and warn that, "Unless the natural desire of children to help and care for others is nourished, they fail to develop a sense of their own value and instead learn to live an empty, self-centered existence" (2000, p. 58).

Generosity is fostered at MMS in a number of ways. MMS provides service learning opportunities for students. Even though more than 70% of MMS's students are eligible for free lunch, they enthusiastically raise money to help others in need. Instructional strategies also foster generosity in the classroom, especially the use of cooperative learning and peer tutoring. The most striking demonstration of how important generosity is in the school setting occurred through the implementation of inclusive education. In particular, when students with more significant disabilities were included in general education, all students had an opportunity to give in many ways.

One example occurred when a student with disabilities read aloud in class. Reading out loud is very challenging for him, but the other students waited quietly and patiently while he read his paragraph. After he finished, the class spontaneously burst into applause. He smiled, and the class knew that he felt great.

The student also gets opportunities to give back to his friends by sharing in their successes and contributing his talents on group projects. One teacher speculated that somehow the student's peers were just a really special group of students. Then, he thought for a minute and said, "No, I think they are different because [the student] is in the classroom."

When MMS teachers watch students interact in such generous and positive ways, they are often moved to tears. Unfortunately, teachers in most schools are more used to focusing on negative behaviors, especially for middle school students. When they witness students being generous to one another, they can change their attitudes toward inclusion, and this spirit of giving ultimately results in more positive interactions in the classroom and school.

INTO THE FUTURE

The principles of the Circle of Courage help sustain the leadership and staff at MMS as they continue with systemic school change and as the inevitable challenges arise. Change is always difficult, but implementing smaller democratic learning communities, positive behavioral supports, and inclusive education have all contributed to a positive school culture that values belonging, mastery, independence, and generosity. Next year, MMS will welcome back neighborhood students with significant disabilities who have traditionally been bussed across the city to self-contained programs for students with intensive support needs. The school staff is excited yet apprehensive as they prepare to welcome these students into an inclusive school environment. Inclusion of students who need intensive supports will be a new chapter for MMS, but the staff will continue to be guided by the Circle of Courage and will heed the words issued by Van Bockern et al. that "Reclaiming children requires each educator to be courageous and willing to struggle with imperfect systems in order to make sure that belonging, mastery, independence, and generosity are made available for all children" (2000, p. 73). This school community welcomes the challenge.

Memories Middle School
Accountability Card # _____
Start Date: __/__/__   End Date: __/__/__

Name: _____ ID#: _____
Home Phone #: _____ Cell Phone: _____
Parent: _____ Work Phone: _____
Parent: _____ Work Phone: _____

	Consequences	Comments	Date	Teacher	Parent Signature
1.	Verbal Warning				
2.	Student Response Form				
3.	Parent Contact • Phone Call • Mail • Counselor Referral				
4.	EPSS Conference BIP and/or AIP				
5.	Administrative Referral				

Dress Code Violations						
Date	Violation	Warning	Sent to Office	Parent Contact	Teacher Initials	Parent Initials

Period	Teacher/Class
1	
2	
3	
4	
5	
6	
7	
Lunch	A B C

Figure 17.1.   Middle school accountability card. (*Key:* AIP, academic improvement plan; BIP, behavior intervention plan; EPSS, educational plan for student success.)

Key:	1) Tardy		2) No Supplies		3) No Assignment		☺ Character Counts		

Week 1 Date ____	Period 1	Period 2	Period 3	Period 4	Period 5	Period 6	Period 7	*Teacher Initials*	*Parent Initials*
Monday									
Tuesday									
Wednesday									
Thursday									
Friday									
Comments:									

Week 2 Date ____	Period 1	Period 2	Period 3	Period 4	Period 5	Period 6	Period 7	*Teacher Initials*	*Parent Initials*
Monday									
Tuesday									
Wednesday									
Thursday									
Friday									
Comments:									

Week 3 Date ____	Period 1	Period 2	Period 3	Period 4	Period 5	Period 6	Period 7	*Teacher Initials*	*Parent Initials*
Monday									
Tuesday									
Wednesday									
Thursday									
Friday									
Comments:									

Week 4 Date ____	Period 1	Period 2	Period 3	Period 4	Period 5	Period 6	Period 7	*Teacher Initials*	*Parent Initials*
Monday									
Tuesday									
Wednesday									
Thursday									
Friday									
Comments:									

REFERENCES

Armstrong, T. (2001). *Multiple intelligences in the classroom* (2nd ed.). Alexandria, VA: Association for Supervision and Curriculum Development.

Brendtro, L.K., Brokenleg, M., & Van Bockern, S. (1990). *Reclaiming youth at risk.* Bloomington, IN: National Educational Service.

Johnson, D.W., Johnson, R.T., & Holubec, E.J. (1993). *The new circles of learning: Cooperation in the classroom and school.* Alexandria, VA: Association for Supervision and Curriculum Development.

Kunc, N. (2000). Rediscovering the right to belong. In R.A. Villa & J.S. Thousand (Eds.), *Restructuring for a caring and effective education: Piecing the puzzle together* (2nd ed., pp. 56–76). Baltimore: Paul H. Brookes Publishing Co.

Tomlinson, C.A. (2001). *How to differentiate in mixed-ability classrooms* (2nd ed.). Alexandria, VA: Association for Supervision and Curriculum Development.

Van Bockern, S., Brendtro, L.K., & Brokenleg, M. (2000). Reclaiming our youth. In R.A. Villa & J.S. Thousand (Eds.), *Restructuring for a caring and effective education: Piecing the puzzle together* (2nd ed., pp. 56–76). Baltimore: Paul H. Brookes Publishing Co.

18

He Called Me Duffy

Frances R. Duff

I first met Phillip when he became part of my yearbook staff in the fall of 2001. He wheeled into the yearbook room, crashing into the doorframe, a desk, and two chairs. He made quite an entrance, to say the least! The rest of the students on the staff took note of his arrival—there was no way to avoid it—and waited for me to introduce him and the other new students who entered more demurely. We had been waiting for Phillip's arrival for weeks. After brief introductions, the new students were welcomed into the editorial teams and were shown the ropes by the senior staff. This moment was an important one for me.

I was a general education teacher with limited experience in inclusion. Prior to my year with Phillip, the only students in special education whom I had encountered in my classes were those with specific learning disabilities. As I sought support from a colleague, she mentioned in passing that there were students with more significant disabilities on campus. This information was a revelation. In fact, I had to take it on faith. I had not seen any students with intensive support needs in my previous 7 years at this school.

I was aware that many special education students were educated in self-contained classrooms. I was unaware, however, of the alienation this segregation engendered in the students. I became aware of it quite suddenly when we distributed the "Senior Superlatives" questionnaire. Typical of most high school yearbooks, ours included a section of students chosen by their classmates as "most popular," "most likely to succeed," "best athlete," and "biggest flirt," among others. In one of the classrooms, just a few doors down from mine, a self-contained English class refused to take part in the survey. One of the students summarized the feelings of his classmates, "Why should we vote for any of them? We don't even know who they are!"

How could I have known that this group was so removed from the school community that they didn't know the most prominent students in the senior class? How could they have spent close to 4 years at the school without becoming aware of the students who served in student government, starred in the school plays, or played on the basketball team? If the students with invisible learning disabilities were excluded from school activities, where then did that leave those students with multiple or severe disabilities? I was beginning to realize the chasm that separated special education from general education. It distressed me that I was part of the system that prevented these kids from enjoying the activities and events of the high school community.

As the sponsor of the school's yearbook, I recognized an ideal opportunity to "uncover" the hidden populations of our school. The yearbook was the ideal class for students who were segregated from the general education population. What better way to become part of the school community than to be a member of the prestigious yearbook staff? It took me 4 years to convince the special education department to allow me to have students with extensive needs in my yearbook class.

I am convinced that their reluctance was due to apprehension. The students who I requested were sheltered in classes where they were protected from the pitfalls of high school social situations. The teachers may have feared that the students would not be welcomed in regular education classes. Apparently, before I asked, no one had expressed the desire to include kids with significant disabilities in their classes. It just took the right confluence of stars and talking to the "right" people to make this inclusion class happen. I am still grateful to the special education teachers and administrators who trusted me to undertake the care and education of these students who were leaving behind the security of their special education room.

When Phillip and his classmates finally became members of the yearbook staff, I had cause for celebration. I also had cause for high anxiety. I expected to be under a powerful microscope. If I failed, then my students would be relegated again to a second-class status in the school community. If they were to be welcomed into other general education classes, I would have to prove that they were successful in mine. I knew that what I did or did not accomplish during this year would make a difference in the lives of my students.

What I had not anticipated, however, is the difference this year would make in my own life.

Once Phillip got over being the "new kid" in class, he quickly joined the rather raucous activities of the yearbook staff. Under relatively controlled conditions, chaos reigned. The yearbook room was consistently hectic. Students were involved in countless simultaneous activities. Phillip became a buddy to one of the senior staff members and accompanied him often on his photographic outings. They became an invaluable team, working together on layouts and finding ways to keep the class upbeat and giggling. Laughter rang continually from the room, and Phillip's sense of humor and his uncanny timing were often its source.

I realized soon after Phillip's arrival that he was one smart individual. No one could be as quick-witted and funny as he was unless he was bright. I was outraged to discover that Phillip was not included in any other general education class. Yearbook was his *only* contact with the general education students. I vowed to rectify that injustice in the ensuing school year.

Phillip now became a familiar sight in the school corridors. He was a quick study and learned how to take advantage of his position as a working member of the yearbook team. He volunteered often to take on tasks outside of the classroom. In a large, comprehensive high school, there is privilege attached to being able to leave the room during class hours. Only the "distinguished" students had blanket hall passes, and Phillip had earned the right to be a member of this widely envied group.

Phillip and his buddy ran frequent, and often suspiciously time-consuming, errands. The tray on Phillip's wheelchair became a useful vehicle for delivering sets of questionnaires to other classes. He also discovered that it was a convenient carrier for vending machine snacks and sodas. His teammate and he sometimes left the classroom with a stack of papers and a cache of money and returned fully laden with provisions for the afternoon.

In addition, the halls, devoid of other students, became a speedway for Phillip's chair cranked up to its highest level. I threatened to post speed limit signs on the walls. Beneath my tough exterior (which, by the way, he saw through immediately) lay an exultation that Phillip now belonged to the school community in his own, mischievous way.

What a year! By the time the yearbook was finished, I had learned a great deal about my students, especially my seniors and Phillip. There is a unique bond that develops between a sponsor and her editors. Conversations become more personal, and topics become more heartfelt. The yearbook ambience changes from day to day, much like the proverbial roller coaster. Deadlines exact their unyielding tolls on students. Feelings run high, sliding overnight from the exhilaration of a completed layout to the dismal disappointment when the computer "loses" 2 days' work. Relationships become more intense, and the teacher finds herself intrinsically linked to the welfare of her students.

Some of my yearbook students were moving on to college and other postsecondary pursuits, but Phillip had 2 more years of high school. I would have time to know him even better. During the next 2 years, I would have the opportunity to ensure Phillip's inclusion in general education to a greater extent. I felt compelled to unwind the red tape that had kept Phillip tied up in segregated settings. Watching Phillip take control of his responsibilities in yearbook convinced me that he could handle taking on a class full of seniors.

I convinced Phillip's support teacher to enroll Phillip in my senior humanities class for the following year. That year proved to be a turning point in my career. Suddenly, I found that despite my many years of experience, I had discovered an entire universe of students who had never really been visible before.

Special education found a permanent niche in my psyche, and I was determined to build on the success of the previous year. On the first day of the semester, Phillip entered the room with his usual panache. He arrived while the rest of the class were being subjected to the usual, opening week monologue about rules, and supplies, and expectations, and blah, blah, blah. The students were in a stupor after a long summer break and were blearily still. Phillip crashed through the door, drove into the doorframe, banged into a desk, backed up, crashed into the doorframe again, sideswiped another desk and planted his wheelchair in the middle of the room. The students were startled by the commotion. With all eyes turned toward him, Phillip blurted out, "I need airbags!" We were done for. The students and I laughed uproariously, and the awkward moment of silence was gone.

Phillip's personality and his sense of humor set the tone for the rest of the year. Laughter would again ring from my classroom. Phillip brought honesty and joy with him wherever he went. I was fortunate that he added his energy to my classes. My days were brightened by his cheerful smile and the nickname he coined for me. He called me Duffy, and perhaps that name was the beginning of a new persona for me. I wanted to be a student again and to find a way to demonstrate to other teachers that "those" kids belong in the same classes as "regular" kids.

Once again, although under different circumstances, my class became a team. My general education students had not been in classes with kids with significant disabilities before; yet, they were nonplussed by the inclusion of Phillip and two other students who needed assistance. My faith in my students' sensibilities was rewarded. Liz Keefe, one of the co-editors of this book, told me many times that "the kids make it work." Time after time, I have seen the truth of her statement in the attitudes and behaviors of my students.

Our class had disability awareness infused in the curriculum. Phillip became a resident expert on certain disabilities and the effects they had on the lives of students. He raised our awareness of the obstacles that the world put in his path. Phillip's disability became unimportant to his friends unless their sense of social justice was offended. They became advocates for universal design and spoke up boldly when they noticed violations. They learned to see their environment through Phillip's eyes, and their view will never be the same again.

In an effort to provide more therapeutic time without reducing his time with his classmates, Phillip's educational assistant and I undertook the task of placing Phillip in his stander during class. We both overestimated our skills. Trying to be inconspicuous, we chose a moment while the students were reading a short assignment to lift Phillip from his wheelchair and strap him into his stander. Instead of a subtle change of position for Phillip, we provided the entire class with a farcical comedy performance reminiscent of the Marx Brothers in a steamship stateroom. Phillip started laughing at our incapacity; the class started laughing at us, too; and we just bumbled on until Phillip was secure. We repeated the process in reverse a few minutes later, much to the delight of Phillip and his classmates.

A great deal of good-natured teasing was our lot for a few days. Students entered the room asking if we had dropped Phillip yet. Other students reminded Phillip that he should require his teacher and his educational assistant to take remedial "stander" lessons. All in all, the fun the kids had at our expense added to the sense of teamwork that was developing. I was truly moved by Phillip's trust in me. He knew that I would work until we could make the transfer smoother and less conspicuous. He was patient and understanding, although he did remind me that I was a *klutz*.

What was remarkable about the scene was that the class laughed at the comedy of errors created by two inept adults. They were laughing at me, not at "the kid in the wheelchair." Here was a group of students who would never join the crowd in taunting a person with a disability. They were not afraid to laugh at us because they knew that we would not misinterpret their amusement. We all knew each other well enough to understand that laughter is not necessarily linked to mockery. Given the opportunity to prove themselves, students have open and generous hearts. With guidance and encouragement, all young people can see beyond superficial differences. As a teacher, I was bursting with pride in the character of my students.

As part of a career exploration, Phillip was assigned as an assistant to the technology coordinator at a nearby elementary school. I stood aside as he demonstrated his sense of responsibility and his growing independence in his work away from the high school campus. Sometimes, as I watched him leave the school building, I felt like a mother robin watching her fledgling jump from branch to branch. I was beginning to acquire a better understanding of my role. I had taken Phillip under my wing, but I was obliged to let him fly on his own. I was learning to step back and allow Phillip to take risks so that he could earn his independence.

As the school year ended, I met again with Phillip's support teacher and, together with Phillip, we made plans for his senior year to include four periods of general education classes. I knew that Phillip needed to break away from me, and I told him so. He had been with me now for 2 years for a good part of each day. If he was to journey out into the world, he needed to expand his experiences in high school. I assured him that I would be there if he needed me. I knew he was scared. I had become his "guardian" in general education. He was comfortable with me and felt secure in my classes.

To be honest, I was afraid, too. The "what ifs" flooded my imagination. What if he didn't make friends in his new classes? What if the teachers did not encourage his classmates to be accepting? What if—I just let go? I heard in my own doubts the echo of the myriad excuses that had been offered for keeping Phillip in a self-contained class. I wanted Phillip to become as independent as possible. I would not allow my fears to hold him back.

We reached a compromise. He would take a communication skills class with me and enroll in three other general education classes besides mine. We would still be able to maintain contact, but he would have to become his own advocate in his other classes. I put my faith in his self-determination and allowed him to stretch beyond his comfort zone.

Phillip was one of a handful of seniors in a communication skills class that is typically part of the sophomore curriculum. For many reasons, some students wait and add it to their senior schedule. As an upperclassman in a tenth-grade class, he joined the other seniors

He Called Me Duffy   133

in developing a cocky attitude. I knew Phillip too well and just waited until the air of superiority blew over. He was just too friendly to allow a façade to interfere with his relationships; however, his senior status did offer him a few privileges to lord over the other students. In addition, he was an office aide during one period of the day and had the run of the corridors again.

Phillip's status among his classmates grew daily. He developed a close friendship with one of the senior boys in the class. Under the guise of completing a lengthy assignment, they would ask for a pass to use Phillip's voice-activated computer in a different class-room. Apparently, there was a good deal of voice activation between them, but not so much between Phillip and his computer. The quality of Phillip's work declined.

I found myself in a quandary. I delighted in Phillip's newfound friendship, but I knew that he was falling behind in his academic progress. I had to find a balance between social growth and academic competence. I put on my "mean" hat and recorded a *D* on his report card. He had never earned a low grade before because he had never been held accountable for his work. He received good grades because so many others had based his grades on sympathy rather than accomplishments. I realized that there is a kind of prejudice in that, too. Others had consistently underestimated Phillip's abilities and, in doing so, denied him chances to prove himself.

That *D* had a marked impact on Phillip's work ethic. Assignments were now completed thoughtfully, and his grade improved based on merit. When Philip saw his semester grade of *B*, he knew he had earned it. The grade was a reflection of his hard work, not an appeasement of his disability.

I was getting smarter, too. I saw in myself the resilience I had wanted to foster in Phillip. I risked damaging our relationship in order to allow him to take more control over his own behavior. I stood fast in the face of the near tears when Phillip read his earlier report card, and now I could grin at the twinkle in his eyes as he beamed over his semester grade. Phillip had made academic strides, but I had learned a great deal more about myself and the direction I wanted my career to take. Somehow, I decided, I would provide a springboard for students with disabilities, a jumping-off place for them to take on the world with as much grit as they could muster.

With the arrival of spring, high school seniors become a bit daffy. Phillip was no exception. I discovered him and his friend ditching a class. I scolded both of them and wrote the appropriate referrals, but behind their backs I celebrated Phillip's rite of passage. Truly, now, he had joined the ranks of the typical teenager. As the semester drew to a close, Phillip occasionally *extended* his lunch hour when he went off campus with his friends. I found out about his outings accidentally when I overheard them talking to some of their classmates in the hall. I knew how difficult it had been the previous year for another student in a wheelchair to get permission to leave campus. Phillip had not even asked for permission. He was a senior; seniors were allowed to leave campus; therefore, Phillip left campus. I could see that he was no longer an outsider.

My role became less and less important in his growth, and, though I knew I would miss him, I was happy to see him lose the last vestiges of his dependence on me. He was well on his way to a more independent life in the community beyond high school. His charm and his sense of humor would serve him well, but his growing sense of competence would serve him even better.

I look back on those first few weeks and realize that as Phillip barreled into the yearbook room, he also crashed his way into my heart. He taught me how to teach in a way no university classes or former students had done. He forced me to see myself in a new light. My role as a teacher became that of a guide, urging my students to become who they are, not what I want them to be.

Phillip showed me that I had become complacent as a teacher. He challenged me to pursue a new dream. Instead of looking toward retirement at an age when this is the usual goal, I am beginning a brand new phase of my career reaching beyond what I know. Like Phillip, I am barreling at full throttle into a new environment. Every new experience challenges my assumptions about education and offers me an opportunity to create an atmosphere that invites all kids to learn. Phillip and his classmates taught me that boundaries and obstacles are meant to be surmounted. I expect no less of myself than I expect of him; we both can conquer life without airbags.

19

We Can Do More
Things than We Can't Do

Phillip Contreras (as told to Veronica M. Moore)

I couldn't believe it when she told me the news. "How would you like to go to Boston?" my teacher asked. Was she crazy? Did she think I would say no? "Of course," I yelled, practically falling out of my chair. If you could imagine someone who uses a wheelchair jump for joy, that was me at that very moment.

"Don't you want to know why you're going to Boston?" she asked. Actually, I didn't care why—I was being given a chance to fly across the United States to visit somewhere I've only read about. A place that is mentioned in the history books. A place that actually had a professional sports team. And even better—I was going without my mom and dad. Could life be any better for a 16-year-old?

When I finally calmed down, my teacher explained that the University of New Mexico gave me an all-expense-paid trip to give a presentation at the TASH conference in Boston, Massachusetts. TASH is a group that helps people with disabilities be included in school and in the community. This was perfect since I want to be a motivational speaker when I graduate from high school! I love to talk, and I have been giving presentations about inclusion since I was in middle school. I have cerebral palsy, and I have taught other kids and teachers about what that is and why it is important for kids like me to be included in regular education classes.

Even though I have already given lots of presentations at schools and at the University of New Mexico, this time I knew my speech would have to be different. I had to make people from all over the nation realize why kids like me needed to be included in regular classes. I had to think about what was important for new teachers to know and decide what I could say to make them really understand how important inclusion is.

If you don't know what inclusion is, it is where kids with disabilities are included in regular education classes with kids without disabilities. I feel pretty strongly about this issue because I never was really included until a couple of years ago. I always had my classes in the portables far away from the regular kids. Since I have cerebral palsy, people thought I couldn't really do anything else outside of a special education class. My teachers in middle school had me in a CBI (community-based instruction program). All of my classes were away from the other kids. Part of that class taught us about public speaking. So I got to go to other classrooms and tell the kids in regular ed. about cerebral palsy.

Even though I got excited before each presentation, I would sometimes get sad, too. I used to look around and wish I could be in there with them. I wanted to get the chance to do all of the things they were doing in there, like reading interesting books, conducting science experiments, or even just hanging out. One time when I was giving my lecture, I wondered . . . if I'm good enough to speak to the kids in these classes, why can't I be in these classes? No one had a good answer to explain why I wasn't allowed in there. I was always just told that my skills weren't high enough or that I needed to be in a class where I could learn how to live in the community.

Well, when you're in middle school, your school is your community, isn't it? This was the first time I really felt left out. My teachers were always nice and did what they thought was best. I don't ever want to fault them for that. But, maybe if they would have let me get out of special ed. for some of the day, have some regular friends, and let me into the regular class, things would have been a lot different for me.

Inclusion is good for so many reasons. I hated the work I did in my special education classrooms. I always felt like I could do so much more. I wanted to learn about the subjects the kids in regular ed. studied, especially history. I used to get so frustrated because I wasn't allowed to do the same things as the other kids. Sure, I got lots of extra attention at school, and I'm even allowed to break some rules, but I always thought the teachers and other kids were kind of afraid of me because of my CP (cerebral palsy).

When I was preparing for my TASH presentation, my teachers asked me lots of questions to get me ready. One of them was about my first experience in a general education class. It was when I was in tenth grade. I was in the yearbook class. At first, it was really scary. No one would talk to me. I had to make jokes and be the outgoing one. Since I don't use my arms that much, I was worried that there was nothing for me to do in that class, and I was frustrated. Here it was my first time in a regular ed., class, and it was yearbook even . . . a class that most kids kill to get into, and I felt useless.

I almost wanted to give up until my teacher saw that I wasn't getting as involved as I should have. She moved me to another table and found jobs that I could do. I actually began doing things and contributing to the class. She teamed me up with this guy named Keyan. He and I would help each other. He would cut things out for me and explain what we were going to do, and I would make his computer work every time he broke it (and it broke a lot).

People were always surprised that I know how to fix computers. I've been around assistive technology all of my life. In fact, I couldn't have made it through school without it. Those are the type of things that people don't understand about me and probably others with disabilities. We can do more things than we can't do. The only thing is that we do them in different ways or just need some more time to get the job done. Just because it takes a little bit longer doesn't mean it's impossible. For example, I take a long time to talk. That doesn't mean that I don't have anything to say.

My yearbook teacher saw that I had a lot to say, and she made time to talk to me all the time. She got to know me pretty well, and I used to tease her a lot. She put me in her Vision 21 class. Vision 21 is a class where you learn English, history, and get a mentorship. Vision 21 was the best thing that ever happened to me. A whole new world finally opened up. For the first time, I was really a part of a regular education class, not just a guest. My teacher let me do my physical therapy in the class. She made me feel like every other regular kid, even if it was when I was in my stander or crashing into desks because my wheelchair speed was too high. I finally felt accepted and knew people were listening to what I had to say as a member of the class. Finally, I was learning how to be successful in a real community—regular education.

Even though I feel like I've been lucky about getting out of special education classes all day, I don't think many other kids with disabilities have had the same opportunities. It's not fair that people automatically judge you because of the way you look or the way you speak. There's so much that I wanted to tell teachers. That is why I was asked to give the presentation at TASH.

After thinking about some of my school experiences, some of which I just shared with you, I finally was ready to go to Boston. I worked so hard on my presentation. Trying to pick out the right words to say, reminiscing about great and not-so-great memories, and practicing the speech about a million times had left me exhausted and kind of frustrated. "Now, it's time to relax," my teacher said when we were in the airport. My speech was polished, I had my ticket in hand, and I even thought I was a little bit scared. I figured she might be right. The hard part of preparing was over. Now, all I had to do is kick back and enjoy the flight.

Let me tell you, bro, my travel nightmare was just beginning. We left on that cold, December morning, and I remember feeling really nervous, yet excited. Have you ever been on a plane with someone in a wheelchair? At first, I thought it could be cool since we got to cut in line. But, the chairs don't fit down the aisle in the airplane. I had to be carried by two guys who worked for the airplane. That was kind of embarrassing, but what can you do?

The worst part is that they never even talked to me. They asked my teachers if I was comfortable. I was like, "Hello—I'm right here; I think I can answer that question" I got settled, and actually it was a pretty good seat. "Well," I thought, "at least it will get easier now." Even though we almost missed our connecting flight because of the inaccessibility issues, the fact that Boston ran out of accessible taxi cabs, and our "handicapped" hotel room was too small, all in all the TASH conference was a pretty exciting adventure.

While all the accessibility issues were a pain, they were just other points that prove why inclusion is important. If kids with disabilities were included from an early age, maybe more people would understand the struggles and frustrations we have to go through on a daily basis. Maybe if the guy who put me on the plane knew more about cerebral palsy, he would have looked and talked directly at me instead of looking past me and talking about me to my teachers.

The advice I shared at the presentation and the advice I want to share with you is simple. No one should be separated because of the way they look, act, or because of any type of disability. The law says it, and my experiences have proved it. I have learned so much more about history, books, and how to get along with people because I have been in regular education classes. Now, I feel that I could go to college. If I didn't have the chance to be in regular education, I probably wouldn't feel the same way.

I also like to believe that I taught the kids without disabilities a new way to think. Before they met me, they may have been scared of people with disabilities. But I've shown them that cerebral palsy is not frightening, and I've hopefully opened their minds. Who knows? Maybe some of my classmates will think of me when they're designing a new building or business and do it a totally new way.

20

It Has Nothing to Do with Being Smart

Alex Weatherhead

I first got into special education in the fifth grade. Someone from administration would take me out of class when there was testing. Sometimes, the teacher would not let me leave the class because she thought it was not appropriate. In seventh grade, I got out of special ed. but was put back in during my sophomore year.

I think special education classes taught me to get along better with my classmates and even allowed me to get close to them. At that point in my life, it was a very big step for me.

Everyone in special ed. has a disability. Many people have an image of special ed. as only people with major disabilities that everyone can see. Some people in special ed. just need more time on tests or work better in small groups or are dyslexic. The purpose of special ed. should be to help students to focus more and to do better in school.

The other day, I was sitting in my business applications class with my best friend. My teacher asked me if I was in special education. I answered yes, but my best friend answered, "No, she's not. She's smarter than I am." I told her that it has nothing to do with being smart or not. I told her that I have attention deficit disorder and cannot work in large groups because it causes anxiety.

I thought long and hard about our conversation. My friend had a stereotyped image of special education. I did not meet her expectations. She had just learned something new about me. She came with me as a guest speaker to teacher preparation classes at the university.

For a long time, I would not tell anyone I was in special education. After coming to my current high school for my sophomore year, I found a way not to let it bother me. People are going to think what they want, no matter what.

My high school classes were useful in some ways in dealing with my learning disabilities. But they were also a disappointment because I had the same teachers for sophomore and junior years. They taught me the same thing each year. It was nothing new to me. Some of the special education teachers were condescending and would try to make me feel like less of a person because my learning skills were different.

My support teacher during my senior year convinced me to go into a regular English class. I was really afraid that I would not be able to do the work, but she said she knew I could. The regular ed. teacher, my support teacher, and I met before I transferred in. We agreed that if at the end of 2 weeks I didn't want to stay, I could go back to my self-contained classroom. I decided to stay but was still nervous all the time about not doing well. The reading was harder than I had been used to, and sometimes I got behind. But I had lots of help and earned a *B* in the class for the semester.

Special events and clubs were a way I found to fit in, but they were not enough. I wasn't interacting with good, influential, positive people. I started talking to officers in the Business Professionals of America and joined the association. It had a positive effect on me, and I became an officer during my senior year.

Special education has had both positive and negative effects on me. But here I am now, ready to graduate, an event I have been waiting for since my freshman year.

21

Differentiating Instruction at the Secondary Level

Frances R. Duff

There are a number of truisms that have infiltrated education over the years: *All children can learn. All education is special education. Good teaching is good teaching.* One fact that is often overlooked about truisms is that they are true! As school populations change and teacher training scrambles to keep up with those changes, these statements become clichés and lose their effectiveness to inspire and guide teachers in the practice of their craft. A brief examination of each statement can reveal what has become a lackluster set of ideals for the current secondary classroom.

All children can learn. As it should be, the natural response is "Of course, they can," but the classroom is not always the place where such learning is fostered. Classrooms, especially at the secondary level, have often become repositories of static information, and teachers, the vehicle for delivery of intransigent facts and rigid strategies. A quick perusal of educational standards or a cursory examination of the scope and sequence of course requirements provides an underpinning for the practices of secondary teachers. Within the traditional high school structure, teachers feel obliged to provide the maximum information in a limited amount of time. The result is that "all children" must be modified to "all children who can remember a large body of information delivered through lectures."

All education is special education. It is difficult to find a teacher who does not describe his or her curriculum and methods as deserving of the approbation implied in the word *special*; however, teachers are not prepared to encompass the secondary meaning of that term and provide a comfortable learning environment for students who carry with them the labels of special education categories. Teachers who have been well trained and have been successful in their teaching practices are often overwhelmed by the need to reach students with abilities and behaviors that have been previously absent from their classrooms. Coupled with the demands of rigorous curriculum are the emerging demands of modifying strategies.

Good teaching is good teaching. In the past, teachers' abilities have been evaluated on the *comparative* success of their students. What has rarely been clear, however, is the nature of the comparison. Criteria have varied vastly among schools, disciplines, administrators, and countless other programs and trends in American education. Additional professional development opportunities addressed particular educational issues but seldom provided new insights into techniques and strategies that accomplished teachers could add to their daily practices.

The reality of classrooms today is that there are students with many different learning styles and abilities. Teachers need to address those differences by adjusting their strategies to meet the needs of their students. Perhaps they need to examine the curriculum with a more critical eye to see the relative significance of facts and processes. Key ideas and themes can be developed to allow more students to engage the material in ways other than the regurgitation of facts. As teachers plan lessons, they can examine strategies that allow students to deal with ideas and their interrelationships rather than just expanding their memory functions. The assessment tools that teachers use can reflect their students' strengths in manipulating their knowledge rather than merely passing a test.

Tomlinson has given teachers the framework to build curriculums and develop strategies that provide effective instruction to all students. She defines the process, "At its most basic level, differentiating instruction means 'shaking up' what goes on in the classroom so that students have multiple options for taking in information, making sense of ideas, and expressing what they learn" (2001, p. 1). Using Tomlinson's foundation, we can reenergize these educational clichés to substantiate the truth that formulated them originally.

WHAT DOES A
DIFFERENTIATED CLASSROOM LOOK LIKE?

Classroom environment

- The classroom should be accessible to ALL students.

- In a differentiated classroom, there should be flexibility in seating arrangements. The students should have options other than the usual straight rows of desks. Students should have the opportunity to move to small-group settings frequently.

- The classroom displays should speak to many of the occupants of the room. Look for curriculum-related materials such as word walls, relevant pictures, quotations, procedures, and student work.

- There should be clear evidence of understanding and respect for cultural diversity.

- One aspect of the environment that is difficult to assess directly is the atmosphere of trust and respect. Students must feel confident that their efforts are valued and that their responses are an integral part of the learning in the classroom. Mistakes should not only by accepted but also encouraged.

Teacher behavior

- The teacher should be able to engage ALL of the students, not only by establishing eye contact but also in adjusting vocabulary and delivery to meet the needs of the students.

- Lecturing and questioning practices should vary from the typical IRE (Initiate, Respond, Evaluate) model. There should be evidence of students' inquiry into the materials.

- The teacher should interact comfortably and frequently with all members of the class. In addition, he or she should encourage camaraderie among ALL students.

- The teacher can foster good working relationships among the students by his or her attitude and by direct intervention.

- The interactions between the teacher and students should indicate the level of respect that has emerged during the year.

Student behavior

- Students should be engaged in learning. Quiet does not equal learning. Although some activities require a quiet atmosphere, others demand movement and noise.

- Students in a differentiated classroom are learning according to their personal learning styles and intelligences.

- Collaborative group activities should be observed often. The size and function of the groups vary, but ALL students should be included in cooperative groups.

- Students with special needs should be welcomed and assisted without apparent disruption of class routines.
- Cultural differences and learning styles can affect the way a student *appears* to be behaving in the classroom. Not all learning *looks* the same.

The lesson

- The purpose of the lesson should be presented clearly to all of the students.
- The objectives of the lesson should be apparent and allow students to achieve their individual learning goals.
- The lesson plan should allow for differences in learning styles and intelligences, although not every lesson accommodates every style or every intelligence.
- Student materials should be easily obtained by all of the students.
- Handouts should be attractive and legible and relate directly to the lesson at hand.
- Teacher-created handouts should be effective in connecting the material to the current lesson. Often the use of graphic organizers helps students (especially visual learners) process the lesson more effectively. The purpose of each handout should be made clear in the lesson.
- Assessment should match the purpose and activities of the lesson. Students should feel comfortable that what is being taught is what will be assessed. There should be no surprises.
- Students should also understand that assessment is part of the learning and not just a form of judgment of their work as compared with their peers.

SAMPLE DIFFERENTIATED ACTIVITIES

Because high school instruction is inherently bound to subject matter, there is no one description of differentiation that fits all disciplines. Therefore, the following activities are limited in scope.

The Lesson in Context

The following activities are presented as examples from a ninth-grade class in English literature and are merely excerpts from a longer unit focused on the study of *The Tragedy of Romeo and Juliet* by William Shakespeare. Romeo and Juliet and the story of their "star-crossed" love are familiar to most readers. The unit was coalesced under the theme *the individual and society*. This is a fairly common thematic approach in single-subject inquiries and interdisciplinary studies in the humanities. The study of Romeo and Juliet was further conducted to develop individual student responses to the essential question: How do the youth of a society relate to their elders? This question addresses not only cultural and literary evaluation but also the issues that pertain to the individual experiences and values of the students themselves.

Prior to the introduction of these activities in the classroom, the students were involved in studies of the life and times of William Shakespeare; the role of Elizabeth I; the structure and function of the Globe Theater; and the nature of the language in Shakespeare's plays, including an examination of iambic pentameter and the Shakespearean sonnet. The students and teacher had read the first scene together, deciphering difficult passages, explicating double entendre, and learning to identify the characters and the opposing houses of Capulet and Montague.

- *Lesson objective*—Students will develop a familiarity and comfort with the language of Shakespeare. (Note the use of the words *familiarity* and *comfort*. The lesson is not intended to extract specific translations or transliterations from the students.)

- *Lesson assessment*—Students will produce interpretations of selected short passages from the play.

Graphic Organizer and Visual Prompts

Certain distinctive elements of Shakespearean verse will be posted on a wall chart from previous lessons (see Table 21.1). The students will work in teams from a teacher-prepared worksheet to address the dialogue between Benvolio and Romeo (see Figure 21.1). The teacher will work from an overhead transparency that parallels the student worksheets.

Step-by-Step Activities and the Application of Differentiation

The task sheet serves as the fulcrum for the lesson and assessment. It is also preparation for a second phase of the activity that deals

Table 21.1.   Sample information posted in classroom prior to activities

"Shakespeare-isms"	
What Shakespeare might say	What an American student would say
Inverted sentence order	
In the glorious garden of evening sings the sweet nightingale whom thou dotes on.	The nightingale that you dote on sings in the glorious evening garden.
Unusual words	
hath	has
thou	you
doth	does
o'er	over
ne'er	never
sups	eats, has supper

Working with your partner(s) complete the column on the right.

What Shakespeare says:	What it means to us:
Bid a sick man in sadness make his will! Ah word ill urged to one that is so ill. In sadness cousin, I do love a woman.	Romeo admits to Benvolio that he is in love.
She hath forsworn to love, and in that vow Do I live dead that live to tell it now.	He says that she does not love him back, and he is in despair.
The woman who has caught Romeo's eye is ROSALINE.	
At this same ancient feast of Capulet's Sups the fair Rosaline, whom thou so loves, With all the admired beauties of Verona.	Benvolio tells him that his "love," Rosaline will be at the Capulet's party.
One fairer than my love—the all-seeing sun Ne'er saw her match, since first the world begun.	
Romeo sees JULIET at the party.	
O she doth teach the torches to burn bright.	
So shows a snowy dove trooping with crows, As yonder lady o'er her fellows shows.	
Did my heart love till now? Forswear it sight, For I ne'er saw true beauty till this night.	
Look on the board for the "Shakespeare-isms."	

Figure 21.1.   Student worksheet.

Table 21.2.   Step-by-step look at presentation of the activity

Function of each step		Lesson directions	Differentiation
A.	This is an anticipatory activity for a discrepant event.	1. Draw a Valentine heart on the board (or have it already there when the students enter) that reads "Romeo & Rosaline 4 Ever."	Virtually ALL students are familiar with the typical Valentine format. The teacher or a peer buddy can point to the Valentine for students with special needs.
B.	This activity connects with previous knowledge and establishes the background.	2. Review the opening scene (read the previous day) that introduced the feud between the families.	This activity brings ALL students up to date with the events in the play.
		3. Refer students to their notes on Shakespeare's verse. Review briefly the pattern of iambic pentameter.	The activity allows ALL students to check the accuracy of their notes and to acquire information that is needed.
C.	By planning the group assignments, the teacher can facilitate the differentiation of instruction as well as provide modifications and/or accommodations without apparent disruption of the class activity.	4. Assign students to work with one or two partners.	The teacher should assign groups based on his or her knowledge of students' strengths and skills.
		5. Distribute the "Romeo + Rosaline" task sheet.	ALL students have access to the same materials.
D.	By demonstrating the relationship between the words and phrases, the teacher provides a model of "thinking aloud." The students have both visual and auditory reinforcement of the material.	6. Demonstrate the "translation" of Shakespeare's verse in the first row of the sheet.	By taking time to analyze the language carefully, the teacher models for ALL students how to look at the structure and vocabulary of English in a different form.
			It also allows ALL students to see that the "message" that is transmitted can be "decoded" and restated in a more familiar form.

(continued)

Table 21.2. *(continued)*

Function of each step	Lesson directions	Differentiation
E. Students practice the process that has been modeled by the teacher. The teacher assists and discusses responses to extend the demonstration of the analysis of the language.	7. Ask students to point out the connections between American English and Elizabethan English in the second row.	The teacher will define forsworn. Students have the "translation" in the last column and can see the words that are similar to the words from the play. Students who have difficulty can take advantage of the oral responses of the other students and the analysis of the teacher.
	8. Point out the next heading "The Woman who has caught Romeo's eye is Rosaline."	ALL students are directed to a small but, in this case, significant, bit of data about Romeo.
F. Student groups can work independently of the teacher to decode meaning from the passages. The teacher can assist as needed on a more individual basis.	9. Ask students to work with their partners to see the relationship between Columns 1 and 2 as in Step 7.	The teacher can observe the groups as they work and offer additional assistance as needed. It is appropriate here to review special modifications and accommodations for individual students.
	10. Direct the groups to complete Row 4 on their own.	*Note:* In many instances, the careful planning of the group structures provides peer assistance in a natural setting.
G. This seemingly inconsequential step is important for student to see the relevance of the following passages.	11. Point out the next heading "Romeo sees Juliet at the party."	The teacher draws attention for ALL students to the introduction of Juliet into Romeo's life. She becomes the object of Romeo's words.
H. This activity offers continued independent practice and whole-group debriefing as well as ongoing teacher informal assessment.	12. Direct students to work together to complete the chart.	This activity allows students to work together to recreate Shakespeare's message in current vernacular. The selections are shorter and simpler so that ALL students can succeed in reading and interpreting Elizabethan English. Again, a carefully planned group structure makes peer assistance possible and practicable.

Function of each step	Lesson directions	Differentiation
	13. Share the responses with the whole class as in Step 10. Give the students time to adjust their responses or to question you.	Because students have worked with partners, there is a shared responsibility for the resulting "translation."
		ALL students can respond with confidence. Students who choose not to respond are still able to participate by listening to the responses and the teachers's comments.
		ALL students will have correct interpretations for further use.
I. This activity offers assessment.	14. Collect the papers.	Individual worksheets allow the teacher to observe how each student worked on the activity.
		In addition, the teacher can be sure that ALL students have the information needed to continue.

with a deeper understanding of the impetuous nature of Romeo and his relationship to Juliet and the adult characters in the play (see Table 21.2).

SO, WHAT'S NEW?

So, what's new with this lesson? That's the point—there really is nothing new about differentiated instruction. It embraces the three tenets introduced at the beginning of the chapter. A good teacher designs lessons so that all children have the opportunity to learn, and student success is defined individually by the students themselves. The key word in every classroom is ALL. The curriculum and techniques must allow ALL students the opportunity to engage in intellectual and social growth. Therefore, all children really can learn, all education is really special (i.e., individualized) education, and good teaching really is good teaching—in the differentiated classroom.

REFERENCE

Tomlinson, C.A. (2001). *How to differentiate in mixed-ability classrooms* (2nd ed.). Alexandria, VA: Association for Supervision and Curriculum Development.

22

Struggling to Succeed

Breanna Ortiz

For me, it all started in third grade with test after test. "They" said I didn't need to be in special education, but my parents pushed and pushed. They saw what I went through behind closed doors. It would take me forever to do my homework and hours to learn spelling and arithmetic. I kept getting frustrated, and so did my parents. After a long hard fight—and more tests—I was finally accepted into a special education program at the end of my third grade year.

I began the fourth grade ready and eager to learn. The funny thing was, though, that I was ready, but my teacher was not. Just one year from retirement, she was not willing to put in the time and effort I needed to catch up with the rest of the class. Short-tempered and anxious, she pulled me through the curriculum, expecting me to memorize everything she showed me. I studied hard almost every night. I used different methods to try to imprint everything in my brain. I was behind in my multiplication tables, spelling, vocabulary, and cursive writing. I struggled to keep my head above water, and somehow I made it through that year. It was my own determination that kept me afloat.

Fifth grade came fast, and I learned that the "calculator was my best friend"—or at least that was what I was told by my teacher. There was some truth to that statement, in fact too much. The calculator and I were becoming really good friends, too good. I depended on the calculator for everything. It got so bad that I couldn't do my math on paper anymore.

My reading was coming along, but slowly. The teachers started to pull me out of class to go to a special education program. I remember it perfectly, as if it were yesterday. The announcements would end, and the honors kids would leave and so would the special kids. That's what they called us, "special kids." People would talk and point, but I didn't care. I knew that it wasn't important, wasn't something I should worry over. I had my real friends. If others could not accept me for who I was, well then, they weren't my friends.

Middle school took off at lightning speed, and nothing got better. I was put into separate special education classes instead of regular education classes. I was with kids who were destructive and had negative behavior issues. I can remember fights that would break out in the middle of class. It was very different for me to be in such an atmosphere. One of my teachers would even sleep during class, and the students would just hang out and do nothing. I had all As in my classes.

Don't get me wrong. I didn't complain about just hanging out. What kid in middle school would? However, after a while, I got sick and tired of not doing anything every day. I started to miss the challenge I would get in regular education classes. My parents were becoming upset now, too. Through their efforts with the school staff, I was moved out of most of the special education classes and attended regular classes except for English and math. These were special ed. classes. They were still too easy, but the school wouldn't let me out of them.

When seventh grade arrived, I hoped that this year would be different. But, again, I was stuck in the special ed. English and math classes. And to make matters worse, these classes were held in a lime green portable that stuck out on campus like a sore thumb. Only the special ed. kids had classes in the barracks away from everyone else. My classmates would just stare at me as I walked into the portable. Not only was the building atrocious, but the teachers were just as horrible. One of my teachers had odd, frizzy hair, and she smelled funny. Another teacher made me feel uncomfortable all the time. Because of the way he talked to me, I always thought that he was "hitting on me" in some way. All in all, the teachers seemed weird to me and did not offer me much help. I didn't think I was learning anything. I began to hate school, teachers, and the whole special education system.

Just as I was ready to give up, my struggle to learn finally found a new avenue. Working with my parents and my IEP (individualized education program) team, I was able to be assigned to regular education classes again. I had a great teacher who actually wanted to work with me and give me the support I needed to do well in school.

Thankfully, my high school experience has been even better. I have a support teacher to talk to, and she helps me improve in the areas I struggle in. I have improved dramatically in my studies and my test scores. I've taken the ACT test and plan to go to college when I graduate. Some of my senior classes are called inclusion classes. The teachers work together to help all of us to achieve success. They make modifications willingly and offer whatever help we need, whether we are in special education or regular education. Special ed. kids and regular ed. kids work together on projects and activities, and no one knows or cares which student has which label.

I'm grateful for the help I did receive when I had a teacher who cared and understood. I hope one day to help others so they won't have to experience the same bumps that I ran into when I was younger. One thing I found out through all of it was that I know who my true friends are.

23

It's More than Just Paragraphs

Jeremy Mallak

Hello, my name is Jeremy Mallak. I first started to be in special ed. in third grade. My test scores were lower than everyone else's. That is when I was tested and diagnosed with ADD. Attention deficit disorder is a disorder that a lot of people have. It makes people unable to sit still for a long time, and it interferes with their ability to listen. In addition to ADD, I have a specific learning disability that was diagnosed by my IEP (individualized education program) team. A lot of people are put in special ed. because of learning disabilities. This disability causes me not to learn as fast as other people. It also keeps me from taking in a large amount of information at one time.

Having a learning disability has been frustrating for me because I want to learn as fast as everyone else. It's also embarrassing. When I am out with my friends, they see me like anyone else, but when we are in the classroom, they discover that I'm slower. It makes me feel like I can't do my own work when I have to ask for help from other students. This keeps me from asking for help most of the time. It's only when I'm afraid I might fail that I'm forced to get help.

Being in special ed. is good in some ways and bad in others. Some good things about being in special ed. are the one-on-one attention, getting all the help I need, and fewer students in each class. This makes it easier for me to pay attention. In special ed. classes, we get different work. The kids in the classes are at the same level as I am. I get less homework. Another good thing is that when I read in front of everybody, I'm not as scared as I would be in a large class. No one in the special ed. class cares if I can't read very well. Regular ed. students might make fun of me because of the way I read. They will not understand that I have a learning disability

One of the bad things about special ed. classes is that I don't really feel ready for some of the things I have to do to graduate. The classes do not give us what we need to know to understand the ACT test and other tests as well. Teachers in special ed. classes teach the same things over and over again. It seemed as if I never learned anything new. For example, when I was in Ms. T's class, she taught us so much about paragraphs that she forgot to teach us about other good stuff. I think that there is a lot more important information other than paragraphs, like information and strategies for the ACT.

I do have one inclusion class now, world literature. There are a large number of regular ed. students and just a handful of special ed. students. I am able to function here because the other students are nice to me. They help me with my work. The teachers, Ms. D. and Mr. C., make the class less difficult for me by teaching things in different ways. They use different strategies until I can "see the light" through them.

The teachers also make this class fun! They do this through having us work on group activities and handling problems with humor. Mr. C. kids around with certain students and gives them "s***" when they deserve it. Ms. D. is a very nice lady. She is understanding and works with the students to help them be successful. Mr. C. also helps with writing, which is very difficult for me.

The teachers treat us all the same. No one is separated because of special ed. All the kids get help whenever we need it. It's fun to do projects with other students, and I don't worry about being slow because the work is kind of different. I can show what I have learned in different ways. The teachers help with reading, too. They help me to understand what we read.

24

On the Road
to Co-Teaching at
the High School Level

Erin Jarry, Eddie Castro, and Frances R. Duff

Excluding students with disabilities from the general education classroom causes emotional pain and academic loss. The voices of the student authors in this book call to us to change the way we educate all students. They remind us of our obligations to reach beyond the curriculum and to recognize the learning of "life lessons" that our students seek. What message do we send to our students when we segregate our classes according to ability or disability? How can our students see the "mainstream" of our society if all they observe in their schools are the barriers to inclusion that we erect?

There are many teachers who have joined the ranks of their students and have begun to storm the fortress that isolates their students. They have formed coalitions to address the needs of their students to overcome the obstacles that an ingrained system of segregation has imposed. Co-teaching makes a strong statement about commitment to educating all students in the least restrictive environment as well as providing all students with the skills and talents of more than one teacher. In co-teaching situations, teachers have the advantage of teaching from their strengths. By collaborating with each other and with the students, they can develop curriculums that address the academic goals of each student and, at the same time, offer students strategies that will help them succeed on their own. Good co-teachers are models of cooperation and mutual support. In optimum co-teaching situations, all students benefit from individualized education in an environment that allows them to collaborate and support each other.

A co-teaching team must be just that—a team! It requires two individuals who are willing to work closely for a common goal: to help all students, those with special needs as well as their typical peers, to succeed in general education classes. This task can be daunting. The situation requires a kind of marriage that takes place between two teachers, one in which the right hand knows what the left hand is doing. Co-teachers need to know each other's teaching philosophies, classroom management styles, grading systems, and personalities.

In order to avoid resistance to a co-teaching model of instruction, teachers need to address the difficulties that have arisen in the past. The team must dispel the misconceptions that have been developed in the absence of real teamwork and replace them with practices that promote learning for all students in a comfortable and natural setting.

- Special education teachers *do* have enough time to provide support to the students on their individual caseloads and still co-teach a class.

- Special education teachers are *not* educational assistants.

- Co-teachers *share* tedious tasks equally.

- General education teachers and special education teachers are *both* responsible for establishing and maintaining classroom behavior with *all* students.

- As long as special education teachers and general education teachers *work together*, it is not "too hard" to include *all* students.

- Time and resources *do* exist to work with *all* students.

Teachers who enter a co-teaching relationship take a leap of faith, in their partners and in themselves. They must trust that their past experiences and their skills will inform their practice in a collaborative environment. Their success as a team will influence the success of their students.

ERIN'S STORY

Ten years ago, my teaching career began in an inclusive classroom where I co-taught with a general education teacher. It was rough in the beginning because we were both new teachers and were unsure of our respective roles. We both had a love of running, and while training for a marathon, we discovered that our time together allowed us to plan and to establish a system for sharing the responsibility for our students' learning. Although we participated in only one marathon, we continued to run and plan classroom activities. Unfortunately, after 3 years, our co-teaching experience was brought to a close as we both moved to different cities.

My new teaching situation was in a self-contained classroom that could be described as a "dumping ground" for special education students. I had students in my class whose eligibility ranged from mild learning disabilities to intellectual disabilities. A few of my students were labeled as "behavior disordered." I could not understand why "my" students could not be included in general education classes. Gone were the collaboration, shared experiences, and teamwork that I loved so much. I began to feel as if I were an ineffective teacher. I learned quickly of the importance of teachers' assumptions and administrators' support in defining the attitude of the school toward inclusion.

When I finally had the opportunity to co-teach in a general education classroom, the experience was disheartening. It was evident that the general education teacher did not want me in "her" classroom. It was obvious that she didn't want "my" special education students in there either, and she did not hesitate to let them know how she felt. I cannot say which experience is worse, working in a self-contained classroom or working on a dysfunctional team.

The future looks brighter now. I am currently co-teaching with two outstanding general education teachers. Collaboration and teamwork are back! We plan together and share the responsibility for all of the students—no distinctions between "their" students and "mine." I truly enjoy working with teachers who are committed to the assuring the success of *all* students.

EDDIE'S STORY

Having spent 10 years teaching English to students with disabilities in self-contained classes, making a transition to an inclusive setting was rough for me. I was used to small-group instruction and had spent time developing strategies to work with my students, especially on writing. Most of my students had trouble writing a simple paragraph; they had not been required to participate in established writing programs. It was like pulling teeth to get the students to break out a sheet of paper and a pen. "I don't know what to write," and "I didn't do anything last summer," were typical responses.

Eventually, by introducing prewriting processes, I was able to convince them to write in spite of their reluctance. The amount of time I spent with each student was immense. The process of prewriting, editing, and revising seemed to go on for weeks with each essay.

When I made the transition to being part of a team in a general education classroom, I was concerned about providing special education services in a large class where the majority of the students were in general education. This new environment raised the bar for me and for the special education students who were being included, most for the first time, in a general education class. The atmosphere was hectic, and the work came at a much faster pace than we had been used to. There was ample reading accompanied by written responses requiring analysis and critical thinking. I was worried about how the special education students would cope with the assignments. The surprise came when I evaluated the essays from all of the students. General education students had the same difficulty as the special education students in producing a sound essay. Many of their essays lacked thesis statements, omitted introductions and conclusions, and contained numerous run-on sentences or sentence fragments. I understood then that I could bring the skills I had developed during the past 10 years to working with all of the students in this class. My co-teacher and I developed a comfortable balance in the teaching of literature and writing. We both collaborated on assignments and evaluation of student work.

Ms. D., my co-teacher, helped me to succeed in my first experience of inclusive education. She remained patient and proved to be a teacher's teacher. We share ideas about differentiating instruction and direct our efforts toward teaching so that *all* children can learn. I continue to hone my skills, and the learning process for me has only just begun. Ms. D. and I will collaborate for the rest of this year and have more time in the summer months to plan a curriculum for the next school year. Now that I have been involved in co-teaching for a semester, I know the rest of the school year will provide continued success for me and for the students. I hope our collaboration will serve as a model for other teachers to emulate.

FRANCES'S STORY

Working with a co-teacher has become second nature to me. It is difficult to describe the gestalt that develops when two adults are dedicated to the same principles of equity and education. How better to demonstrate cooperative learning than to allow our students to see us collaborating? In a healthy co-teaching partnership, the teachers open their strategies to the scrutiny of the students. My teammates and I have learned to trust not only each other but also our students.

Our students are aware of the differences in our personalities and our points of view. They approach us equally for assistance or just for conversation. They understand that we are a team, and there is no sense of hierarchy in the classroom. In one class, for instance, my co-teacher and I have become accustomed to answering to each other's name. The students see us as interchangeable parts in the workings of the class.

As a veteran teacher, I sometimes have to shake off the cloak of venerability that comes with long experience. Experience can often lead to complacency and an undeserved conviction of the "rightness" of one's opinion. I do not want my co-teachers to be deferential to me; I want them to infuse my practice with new ideas and new strategies. When my viewpoint becomes myopic, I am grateful for the clarity of my co-teachers. Their suggestions for strategies, their assessments of the students' work, and their insights into the climate of the class help me to become a better teacher and, I hope, a better colleague.

I believe that when teachers become a team, the class follows suit. When the ebb and flow of the classroom is open and supportive, students readily support each other. Competition becomes friendly, and collaboration becomes essential. Students have observed my teammates and I take opposite stances on topics that have emerged in class discussions. Following the lead of the teaching team, our students are able to argue issues at an intellectual level without falling into the trap of personal attacks. They hear each other's opinion and counter with their own without denigrating their class-mates' contributions. As teachers, we model behaviors that promote an atmosphere of respect among our students.

There is no separation of special education students and general education students as there is no distinction between the special education teacher and the general education teacher in our classes. I doubt that most of the students are even aware that the teachers come from different educational disciplines. They are simply aware that the course is team-taught, and they have the benefit of two adults to offer them different paths to success.

THE REST OF THE STORY

The authors of this chapter work in teams that include general and special education teachers. The special education teachers work in English classes with Ms. D., who has knowledge and experience in differentiating instruction. In addition, those classes are organized in such a way that there is a real sense of community among the students and teachers. The special education teachers also collaborate in history and law classes with Mr. H. whose style is more traditional but whose attitude is flexible and supportive of all his students. The teachers work together in these classes, planning lessons, discussing modifications and accommodations, refining strategies, and providing additional help and support for *all* the students in the classes. The team approach allows for reflection on the success of classroom activities as well as assessment of student performance.

As this program grows at our high school and more teachers come to realize the benefits of inclusion for all students, we believe that educating students with disabilities in general education classes will become commonplace. We realize, and want others to see as well, what the student authors in this book have shown us: Without full inclusion, our special education students will remain isolated and continue to feel like second-class citizens, and our general education students will be denied the opportunity to observe social justice in practice. There is still much work to be done.

25

Living in a Separate (But Gifted!) World

Amanda Goshorn

The stigma of special education has followed me throughout my life, but not in the way one might think. I have found that the words "special education" have a negative impact on students. When disclosing the label to others, it is usually received with grimaces of sympathy and sincere looks of knowing. Even children come to the awesome realization that the classmate who was once considered "regular" is now "special ed." Now, that student is no longer like the average person and, therefore, appears strange and mysterious.

My kind of special education is one that is not normally associated with the usual definition of a learning difference; however, I do learn differently from most students. As I progressed through my years of school, it became more and more obvious that I would be seen as being different from the others. You see, I was a "gifted" student and, therefore, not treated in the same way as everyone else.

As a young gifted student in elementary school, I only was unlike my peers in that two to three times per week I left the classroom with the other gifted kids. I was sent to another teacher for smaller group sessions of creative brain work and various activities meant to develop our above-average minds. You would think that elementary school children would hardly even notice the disappearance of a few of their classmates for an hour several times a week, but, believe me, they were acutely aware of our absence.

The trip to the gifted room was a mysterious experience to those I left behind in the class. The other kids never knew where I was going or what I was doing. They would ask questions but, being so young and hardly understanding how I was different in the first place, there was never really an easy way for me to explain why I got the privilege of leaving the room when everyone else had to stay and finish their math problems. For all they knew, I was enjoying an extra hour of recess. Needless to say, my classmates became skeptical, and I was confused. I couldn't understand why they had changed. I was the same person; I just sometimes went to another class.

The awkwardness I felt wasn't only from my classmates. Many of my teachers did not seem to know how to work with gifted students. I guess students who are labeled as anything other than average are intimidating to some teachers. For example, one year, I had the teacher who every student begged and prayed to get assigned to for the following year. There were many stories that circled around the school about how wonderful she was and how fun she made everything. I was extremely excited when I went to school on registration day and saw that my best friend, my twin sister, and I, all of us equally gifted, were lucky enough to be assigned to the class that every student dreamed of getting into. I knew then that this year was going to be great.

The three of us were quiet, well behaved, and excelled in all of our school work. We aced every spelling and math test and finished our reading books long before the rest of the class. Though many teachers would have seen this as a good thing and devised ways to challenge us with more advanced material, our teacher didn't know what to do with us. About half way through the first semester, our teacher quit even trying to include us with the rest of the class. We were given our own separate curriculum away from the other kids.

Our classroom instruction now consisted of the three of us in the back of the room with the dictionary, trying to fulfill our teacher's demand that we find spelling words that we thought would be challenging enough to require a test. Mind you, our test would take place during a separate time from the rest of the class.

We were quizzed on the words we chose only once, and then we didn't take another spelling test for the rest of the year.

We no longer used the same reading book as the rest of the class. Now, the three of us each received a copy of Shakespeare's *A Midsummer Night's Dream* to muddle through on our own. This choice of reading material was completely inappropriate for a child my age, and we were forced to suffer through it for an entire semester. As one might guess, with so much free time on our hands, the three girls who used to be quiet and well-behaved became talkative and easily distracted. The year that I thought would be one of the best of my life transformed into a nightmare of boredom and endless reprimands.

Luckily, the gifted class turned into a retreat where I could go to be around people who were just like me. We all thought the same way, struggled with the same problems, and, in the end, enjoyed being around each other so much that we developed bonds that stuck with us through high school. The gifted class provided a creative outlet where I could release the boredom and frustration I had pent up inside. I could actually put my mind to work on something that challenged me and gave me an opportunity to expand my educational horizons. In addition, the gifted class was a refuge where I felt comfortable enough to express my opinions freely. Finally, I could function as a thoughtful and productive student. I only wished I could have the same experiences in my regular classes.

As I moved on to middle school, I was excited about the idea of actually having a gifted class that I could go to and participate in *every day.* In my sixth and seventh grade years, I had gifted science. In my eighth grade year, I had gifted language arts and literature.

Having actual subjects to study in my gifted classes made it even more enjoyable, and I have to say that, even until this day, those classes are the most memorable. I'll always remember them because I had the most amazing experiences. I completed interesting projects, I had teachers who cared, and overall I accomplished so much.

Even though I felt I was finally learning in my classes, the social aspect of school was beginning to shift. For all students, the middle school years are critical in developing relationships with friends as well as status within the preteen society. Those of us who were considered "gifted" were forced to band together as we were alienated from the rest of the middle school cliques. While the others would discuss assignments, tests, and other specifics concerning their classes, none of this applied to the gifted kids. We were pushed into our own world outside of the "average" class. We had our own cliques within what was viewed to be a larger clique of "smart kids" and our own stereotype that afflicted almost everyone in the program.

Teachers and students alike did not understand the meaning of "gifted." To them, we were supposed to be freakishly smart and capable of juggling countless difficult assignments all while being immune to the challenges of a not-so-typical preteen life. Little did they know that we, the "gifted" students, were just as diverse as any regular class of students. We had our fair share of smart kids, not-so-smart kids, overachievers, underachievers, jocks, artsy kids, band kids, orchestra kids, leaders, followers, talkers, and, like me, shy kids. We had bullies and victims within us, in addition to those who persecuted us outside of our gifted comfort zone. All in all, if I could have kept being gifted a secret, I would have. Although I enjoyed what I learned in my gifted classes, being afflicted with the label sometimes made me wonder if it was worth it.

Right about the time I got into high school, being "gifted" started to really take a toll on me. I can specifically remember my classmates coming up to me demanding help on assignments in various subjects and then chiding me when I was unable to help or when the answer I came up with was wrong. Because they knew I was gifted, they assumed that I should have some superpower brain, like a machine that could spit out answers on command in less than 3 seconds flat. It turned out that I fell short of many of my peers' expectations and somehow I even disappointed myself when instances like these happened.

The shame and embarrassment of not feeling as smart as everyone else assumed I should be was relentless. As a result, I enrolled only in one gifted class my sophomore year in high school. I found it was easier to fit in if I just took the standard "honors" and "advanced placement" classes like many of the other students. Later, I took advantage of the out-of-school gifted programs like mentorships or internships, but it was only when the school day was over.

Finally, after an extremely hard junior year filled with exceptionally difficult honors and advanced placement classes, I became a senior. I decided to do the unthinkable and take a "regular" world history class instead of the usual advanced placement alternative. On the first day of school, I walked into the class and saw faces I had never seen before in my life. These people were supposedly my fellow seniors, my "peers" for at least the last 4 years, if not more. At that very moment, I became aware of the effects of my being separated into in the gifted society. I recognized only 3 faces in a class of 40 students. I felt like a stranger in my own school.

I learned quite a bit from my experience as an outsider, though. By sitting through this year-long class, I realized how little nongifted students are challenged in regular classes. It's not fair. "Regular" classes should be harder because I'm sure many of the students would benefit from the opportunities to learn the same things I did in my gifted classes. My appreciation for the stimulation that the gifted program provided me came back just as it was about to fade away. I realized that the gifted program and being considered "special ed." was actually the best thing that ever happened to me. True, I hated being thought of as "different," but I relished the experiences my gifted teachers provided me. I will graduate as 1 of 11 valedictorians, all of whom, strangely enough, were gifted with me.

Though I really do appreciate and feel fully deserving of the honor, sharing it with 10 other people made me realize that I am not special. It showed me that anyone can be valedictorian, which leads me to believe that anyone can be gifted, no matter their IQ or their score on an evaluation. I was provided amazing opportunities because of my label. It is unfortunate that other students were not allowed the same.

My advice for every teacher out there is to treat all students as if they were gifted students. Teach your classes as if they were gifted classes. There is nothing wrong with letting the "average" students collaborate with "gifted" students on creative, interesting, and thought-provoking assignments. I doubt my twin sister, my best friend, and I were the only ones in our elementary school class who would have excelled as a result of a more challenging curriculum. The advice also applies to my ultraboring senior world history course. Although it appeared as if the students seemed to struggle with the information, it was probably because the material was presented solely as an outline on an overhead for an hour straight every day. I don't think the students' apathy stemmed from the fact that they were merely "average."

Teachers need to present an idea as if it were fun and exciting and make it something that the students can really pull apart in their brains. Even if the lesson is about the cause of some virtually unknown war, teachers should find ways to entice the students to learn. Presenting information in a boring manner pushes students away and forces them to shut down. When teachers make each day the same as the last and each assignment as predictable as the next, all that students are unconsciously learning is that history class means it's time for a morning nap or a quick trip to the fast food place across the street, rather than seeing it as time for a captivating look back into our ancestry.

Every student deserves a chance to see what good teaching and individualized education is like. There should be no regular, average education. All students should be allowed to experience opportunities and teachers that can offer an enhanced education. The stigmas and stereotypes that go along with the word "gifted" should be abolished, and every child should have a chance at being above average. Teachers need to reexamine the labels they assign to children and pay more attention to the ways that they educate them.

26

The Evolution of an
Inclusive Elementary School

A Principal's Journey

Bea Etta Harris

This chapter describes a history of Corrales Elementary School. It tells the story of a school that began with many self-contained special education classes and pull-out programs and became an inclusive school with all children with disabilities receiving special education services in general education. How did our school get to this point? Let me share some of the highlights of our journey.

During my first week as principal of Corrales Elementary, the special education staff requested a meeting to discuss assignments for the following year. I expected to meet with six or seven staff members. To my surprise 13 staff members attended the meeting. It was clear to me that too many of our 550 students were being identified with disabilities and placed in very restrictive settings. Most students with disabilities were self-contained or pulled out of general education for special education services. One special education program was team-taught with a general education class.

Our high special education numbers were revealed at this meeting, and I resolved to begin reviewing all files of students with disabilities to determine appropriate placement. I refused to accept that there were a disproportionate number of students who belonged in special education self-contained classrooms. Coincidentally, our school had been randomly selected for an Office of Civil Rights review of the special education and support team files. To prepare for this visit, each special education teacher scheduled a conference with me to share current assessments of their students' progress. In the review process, it became apparent that our one "team-teaching" model seemed to produce the best results in that more students returned full-time to general education from the team-taught inclusive program than from the self-contained special education programs.

There are many success stories I could tell you about, but one experience will always stay with me. This event convinced me that we had to change the way in which we were delivering services to students with disabilities. In one self-contained class, there were two students who were identified as having learning disabilities. The students were on grade level in many areas but were not being included in any activities with general education students. When I became aware of this, the teacher was asked to begin to facilitate the students' inclusion immediately. One week later, upon checking with the teacher about her progress, I learned that no effort toward inclusion had been made. I recruited a fifth-grade teacher to include the two boys in her class.

When the two students, who had been in self-contained special education classes for 5 years, were informed that they were to attend a fifth-grade general education class for math, both boys cried. When asked why, they both said that they were afraid. For these two boys, the social issue of participating in a large class was more frightening to them than their math ability or inability. These two students were ultimately very successful in general education, and they exited from special education. In fact, one of the boys just graduated from high school with a grade-point average of 4.0. We had not done these students any favors by separating them from their peers. The experience of seeing the impact of segregation through these students' reactions was the catalyst for my next decision—I began to dialogue with the special education staff who were still teaching in self-contained classrooms to discuss the benefits of inclusion.

Once the dialogue was engaged, it was discovered that many of the general education staff were willing to co-teach with special education teachers; however, some special education staff did not want to co-teach. One special education teacher said, "I am trained to work with children's deficits. I can meet their needs better in a small class of eight students. Why should I team and have to work with 28 students?" Despite objections, I was determined that all remaining self-contained programs would be inclusive the following year. Segregation was no longer an option. I asked special education teachers to find a general education teammate. I requested that each team submit a written proposal with a program design describing how they planned to team. As a result, four fully inclusive classes were created, one each at the following levels: kindergarten, 1–2 multiage, third grade, and a 4–5 multiage class.

Our next evolution was prompted by the large numbers of students with disabilities in third grade one year, which forced us to move beyond including students through team-teaching. These students could not all be in one co-taught classroom, so we decided to disperse the students with disabilities across all third-grade teachers. The special education teacher became a consultant to all of the third-grade teachers. This change was important because it meant that all third-grade teachers, not just those who decided to team teach, were responsible for all students. This change also resulted in more natural proportions of students with disabilities in general education classes. The following year, the special education staff decided to reorganize the special education program to be more inclusive by dispersing all students with disabilities across each grade level as the third grade had done. Each special education teacher would then serve as a consultant to a grade level.

Although we were making good progress toward including students with mild to moderate disabilities, the following experience with a student named Jenny taught me that we still had a long way to go. A neighborhood family visited the school to decide whether their daughter with disabilities should transfer from a self-contained program for students with intensive support needs at another school to our school. We agreed that their daughter would be a welcome addition to our school.

Jenny attended our school for approximately 6 weeks, in which time we learned that, despite our best intentions, we were not prepared to meet her needs in general education. Our school was overstimulating and overwhelming for Jenny. It was the first time she had experienced large groups of students, a general education classroom with 20 students, and a playground with so many students. She began to exhibit inappropriate behaviors, such as undressing in the restroom and choking students, that were alarming to both students and adults.

No one on staff had the preparation to help Jenny. The parents and the school team sat down to review Jenny's status, and even though the bus ride was much shorter, it was determined that her behaviors at school were deteriorating. The individualized education program (IEP) team sadly decided that Jenny would be better served in a self-contained program in another school. We were not happy with our failure to accommodate Jenny. We did not believe that Jenny was not "includable." The problem was our lack of knowledge and skills. Our experience brought to light several issues that we had to reflect on: 1) willingness alone was not enough to include a child with disabilities; 2) preparation and professional development were needed; 3) district resources were needed; 4) general education students and teachers must be prepared for the inclusion of students with severe disabilities; and 5) a younger student with disabilities might be more successfully included.

The next year, a new family with a first-grade boy registered at our school. The first-grade student, Carl, had special needs. Carl was placed in the 1–2 multiage class. I assumed the general education teacher would be willing to accept Carl as a student because the teacher had teamed with a special education teacher in the past, other students with disabilities in grades 1 and 2 were assigned to her, and she had a full-time assistant assigned to her class, in addition to the resource of a special education consultant for part of each day. However, the first day Carl was in class, he hit another child. The incident so upset the teacher that she went straight to me and demanded that Carl be removed from her class.

This presented a dilemma. Because the special education students had been dispersed throughout each grade, there was no team-taught primary class for Carl. The most logical placement was the 1–2 multiage class, but the classroom teacher did not agree with me. The teacher wept tears of frustration, and I was angry. The teacher received technical assistance about modifications from Liz Keefe from the University of New Mexico, but it didn't help. This teacher just did not want Carl in her classroom.

Fortunately, a first-grade teacher walked into my office and said, "I want Carl in my room. It isn't fair that he be assigned to a teacher who doesn't want him. Still, I'm not asking for him [because I want] to help the other teacher. I'm asking for him because I want him in my room."

During the time Carl was in this teacher's classroom, the teacher documented Carl's language and social development and noted that he was making great progress. There were many instances of Carl's classmates caring for him and being perceptive of his needs. When the classmates learned that Carl was moving to another school because his family was moving to a different neighborhood, they and the teacher cried. This experience was very important because we learned that we could be successful with a child who had intensive needs for services.

Our school has now had experience including many students with all levels of disability, including emotional disorders and severe physical and cognitive disabilities. We have found that with the support of local and national experts we can successfully include students with intensive support needs at all grade levels. Each student leads us to learn more and adjust in order to meet his or her needs effectively. Some of these students have made dramatic academic and behavioral gains compared with when they were in self-contained classrooms at other schools. In addition, we have found that the general education students learn a lot from their peers with disabilities.

Teachers have truly embraced the inclusive philosophy of the school. They often speak of a moment in their teaching that was for them profoundly moving—an epiphany. These moments resulted in more than an attitude change; they were moments of moral outrage. The teachers believed exclusion to be an injustice and inclusion, a right, both ethically and morally. This philosophy helps sustain the teachers though the challenges that naturally occur when implementing systemic change.

The implementation of inclusive practices at Corrales Elementary has been an evolutionary process during a period of several years. The move from the traditional self-contained classes for students with disabilities to including them in the general education population and bringing their services to them has been an ongoing challenge. I believe administrators have a great responsibility to provide leadership and support to their staff, students, and school community. Several lessons have been learned, which might be of help to practicing administrators:

- Teachers committed to being inclusive need a high level of emotional, fiscal, and tangible support. An administrator must make a consistent effort to provide resources—personnel, equipment, and time.

- An administrator must actively seek out resources from the district, state, and university.

- An administrator and staff must be flexible because the program changes as the students and their needs change. The administrator and staff need to be able to live with uncertainty, with the goal of inclusion clearly in mind, but need to be flexible about how they will attain that goal.

- An administrator must have an awareness program on the school's inclusion philosophy, which is introduced to the staff, including new and part-time staff, annually. This philosophy should also be printed in the parent handbook and shared with all parents of general education students who are considering the school for their children.

• An administrator needs to know what resources are available in the district for "low-incidence" students, or students who need highly specialized services.

In closing, I would like to say that the greatest lesson I have learned is that this journey is one that is never over. To continue meeting the challenge of educating all of our students together requires constant reflection, vigilance, and flexibility. The reward is to watch students of all abilities grow and flourish together.

IV

Thoughts for the Future

27

Honoring Student Voice
Through Teacher Research

Kathryn Herr

Changing student demographics as well as school reforms such as inclusion are resulting in very diverse classrooms for educators. As teachers, we are asked to bridge these varying worlds to create classrooms and schools that are effective across a wide array of students. We do this based on our own "meaning making" of what students offer us through their behaviors and words, bringing our best understanding to the situations that present themselves to us on any given school day. Yet despite our best efforts, we all encounter students who continue to puzzle or frustrate us and students whom we feel that we have failed. Sometimes this sense of failing our students seems to be at a larger, systemic level in which we question school or district policies and practices that disenfranchise, perhaps unintentionally, whole groups of students.

Students are often ignored as potential political actors in school reform efforts, despite the valuable insights they have to offer as those who are most affected by educational policies and practices (Wasley, Hampel, & Clark, 1997). Teachers, too, are often left out of the decision-making process involved in school change and reform; their professional expertise and experience are often left as untapped resources in the school improvement conversation. This situation can result in improvement plans that are not organic to the school community or that feel imposed.

Teacher action research stands in contrast to many professional development and school change efforts that are conceived by outside experts and are not context specific. It originates in the authentic questions and quandaries of the teachers themselves. The process honors teachers as professionals who can contribute both to their own problem-solving process and to the larger body of educational literature, should they choose to write about their research for sharing with others. It can also honor teachers—and students—as active agents in improving their own school sites.

Teacher action research is conducted by teachers, sometimes with their students, and can serve as a means of instigating change at both the classroom and systems levels. It often succeeds in bringing to the table perspectives that otherwise might not be solicited, acknowledged, or understood because it uses a cycle of inquiry in which data are drawn from the stakeholders involved in an issue. A plan of action is devised based on the data, and the issues are studied once again to see if the action plans have succeeded. This cycle is repeated as often as it takes to arrive at satisfactory, effective solutions. I revisit this idea of the cycle of inquiry later in the chapter.

This chapter explores the potential of action research both as a means of improving the school experiences of students typically disenfranchised or disadvantaged by the status quo of school practices and as a contribution to the professional development of teachers. In addition, I see action research as a means of larger school improvement. I first lay out my own experience as a teacher researcher and then extrapolate what can be learned about the change process from an action research perspective.

STUDYING MY OWN SCHOOL

It was March, and I was *frustrated.* I was working as a counselor in a private middle school. The school had made great recruitment efforts to balance its student body and, to some extent, had succeeded in attracting diverse students; however, too large a number of the students who had been recruited were not succeeding and were in danger of not being invited back to the school. Admission into the school was competitive, and although the students had passed stiff entrance exams to be accepted, their actual academic performance in the school was not reflective of their demonstrated capabilities.

Although I knew I was working *hard* with a large number of these struggling students, I didn't think I was working particularly *well.* Shouldn't I be seeing better results—fewer students on academic probation—based on my well-intentioned interventions? Why were many in this group of recruited students not succeeding?

Although I was actively reflecting on the problem, I could not say that I was making much headway. I was problem solving, but it felt a bit like stabbing in the dark. I wasn't clear enough myself on all the issues that figured into creating this situation, although different "hypotheses" floated around the school. Most of these theories had to do with blaming the students; the most common characterized the students as "lazy" or as not taking advantage of the opportunities and privilege of a private school education.

I had my own hunches based on what I was hearing in my counseling office. I was hearing stories of not fitting in, not feeling comfortable, and of straddling competing worlds and identities. I decided to more systematically gather data regarding the experiences of some of the students in the school, hoping it would be helpful in both bringing their experiences to the faculty and brainstorming solutions. With this in mind, I turned to the experts on the topic for help: the students themselves.

I asked and received permission from the school's administrator to begin to interview students we had recruited, both those who were struggling and those who were succeeding. As a school counselor, I spent my days with those students who weren't doing well; perhaps I could gain some insights from the students who had been recruited and were doing well, those who had "made it." At the same time, I thought it was important to begin to systematically trace and better understand what I was up against with the struggling students.

I began my interviews with Victor, a Hispanic eighth-grade student I knew well because he was routinely sent to my office by his Spanish teacher. Although a native Spanish speaker, Victor was currently failing his advanced Spanish class. He and his parents had received a letter warning that Victor might not be allowed to reenroll in the school if he didn't bring up his Spanish grade. To further complicate the picture, Victor had recently been diagnosed with attention-deficit/hyperactivity disorder (ADHD) and had started taking medication to help address this condition.

Victor's teacher characterized him as a clown who disrupted class. When I was interviewing him, Victor told a story about the day he got in trouble for refusing to take a seat. He began by listing the names of a number of the Anglo American girls in class, some of whom he considered friends and knew well. But then, he started talking about Eduardo.

"I have a friend in there named Eduardo Francisco Fernandez Gomez—you met him—from Del Rio, and he's Hispanic, and I can relate to everything he's thinking and all that—and yet being put in a position also where I got to decide where I'm going to sit during class—am I going to sit with my friends Jenny, Kaitlin, and Virginia, or am I going to sit with Eduardo? It's kind of frustrating. I just didn't like being put in that situation and having to cope with and deal with distinguishing who I really was—'cause that was really hard because I wanted to be proud of my heritage and Hispanic, . . . and yet then again, I usually—what I do is switch. I go to school, I'm school. Then, I switch. I go home, with the neighborhood kids and I, then I switch to Hispanic—and then, in school, I'll turn around to being an Anglo and being that kind of person. It's like Dr. Jekyll and Mr. Hyde. I kind of didn't like being put in that situation because who was I, Dr. Jekyll or Mr. Hyde? And I had to be Victor, and that's kind of hard for me to do, being Victor, just being the person I was."

Victor's narrative pointed toward issues beyond that of failing a Spanish class. He laid out the dilemma facing him and perhaps other recruited students: the disconnection between his home and school identities. To fit in at school, he left parts of himself behind, working to transform himself so that he would be perceived as just one of the kids at school. He worried that he would not be accepted otherwise. Although the narrative Victor offered had to do with his cultural identity, he could have easily taken up the issue of having ADHD or of being from a low-income family in a wealthy school. Any of these areas potentially marginalized him from the norms of the school culture and were fertile ground for this sense of disconnecting from oneself to "succeed" in the school and be accepted.

In this case, Victor's own understanding was that to be part of the school was to leave behind, at least during the school day, part of his identity. Essentially, he was selecting a seat with the other Anglo American students, but in doing so, he was betraying a student like himself. Solving it the only way he could at the time, he refused to take a seat. In essence, his behavior was announcing to the school that this was too difficult a choice: to abandon his own roots to fit in at this school. It also indicated a lesson he was learning in school—the shame he felt about parts of his own identity.

In terms of my own teacher research, although I felt I knew Victor well, I hadn't known the depths of this sense of disconnection and struggle until I more formally gathered data on his experience at the school. Hearing his narrative, I marveled at the ingenuity of Victor's "solution"—to refuse to sit down because the choice of needing to hide parts of himself to "succeed" at the school raised too much dissonance for him. I began to wonder what other parts of themselves students felt they couldn't bring to the school, what parts wouldn't be accepted or began to seem shameful to them.

As a researcher, I learned things from interviewing Victor that I hadn't considered before. Although I understood his teacher's frustration with his disruption of her classroom, I also understood that his behavior was expressing something that needed to be articulated. Without Victor giving some context to his behaviors, they could be easily misconstrued by his teacher: that he was blowing off the class, that he was challenging her authority, that he didn't deserve to pass the class and be invited back to the school. I began to wonder if Victor wanted to continue at the school or whether the tradeoffs felt too great.

Ironically, the theme that Victor was raising—disconnecting from his home culture and identity to be part of the school—was confirmed a bit later in the study when I interviewed one of the school's success stories. At the time of her interview, Janice was a senior at the school and on her way to an Ivy League college. Although considered a success, Janice related what it was like to never see someone like herself—in her case, an African American woman—included in the curriculum or presented as a role model.

"Everything that you see, all the accomplishments, all of the wonderful discoveries, have been done by someone who is white, so what does that make you if you are black? Where does that leave me? What position does that put me in? . . . If you bring black children in but don't expose them to what they are or you don't let them see what has happened with their history or with their culture, in a way you're saying that their culture isn't important, that their history isn't important. And in a way, you're saying that they're not as important because you don't stress what they are."

I began to wonder who else did not see him- or herself in the curriculum of the school. Who could not imagine him- or herself as successful because he or she had no models of people like him- or herself making contributions? My inquiry was taking me beyond helping individual students to succeed to questioning the culture of the school and the ways we as a school community might need to change in order to invite success from a wider variety of students. The narratives of Victor and Janice, much like the stories told by the students in this book, effectively helped translate "individual" struggles to the larger landscape of issues in the school culture.

The data from my study redirected my own problem solving to one that dealt more with institutional issues than with individual student "failures." I was learning how the systematic collection of data, in this case, student interviews, might inform school reform efforts. I had started from a place of wanting to improve my own professional performance, desiring to learn how to better support students at risk. As I analyzed the data, my goal for the research expanded to include the question of how the institution might change to be a more supportive environment for struggling students. Although surprised that the data had taken me in this direction, I was pleased with the evolution of the research and my own increased understanding of the issues involved. But I had more to learn.

As the data analysis evolved, one theme that became clear was the incredible isolation the struggling students faced. There were really no opportunities in the school for them to discover what were common struggles and experiences among them. When they struggled, the students concluded it was their own individual failure rather than anything to do with the educational context in which they found themselves. They knew what their own individual school days were like—their experiences of feeling misunderstood, isolated, or framed as less than able academically—but they did not talk about these things with each other.

Concurrent with this realization, I was also aware that the data gathering was moving very slowly because I was doing the research during my "free" time during the school day. I gathered a small group of boys and invited them to do a group interview. It was an expedient move, designed to speed up the pace of the research effort, but one that serendipitously proved to be an intervention in itself. After meeting once, the boys asked when they would meet again.

The group continued to meet for 2 years. It was always a site for data gathering. I faithfully tape recorded each session, compiling an archive of sorts of the life of the group. After months of exchanging stories of their experiences in the school and interrogating their own roles and that of teachers and administrators in their struggles in the school, the boys moved on in their conversation. They began to articulate the idea that "it's our school, too," and to talk more about how the school might need to change to make this idea a reality. Because they weren't seeing themselves in the curriculum of the school—echoing much of what Janice had previously articulated— they decided to offer a study group after school as well as a film series. Both of these strategies were designed to provide diverse students with a wider array of role models and readings.

In essence, they themselves were beginning to explore the question What contributions have people like me made? They saw these after-school offerings as a temporary solution while they also lobbied for curricular change in the school. Toward this end, they met with the curriculum committee as well as the head of school to articulate their concerns.

For myself as a teacher researcher, I had not considered that the students could be my partners in the change process. I thought I would study *them* and then help devise interventions *for them.* What I learned from them was that students could partner in the creation of schools that are good places for them to learn. I discovered that they not only have things to *say* about their education but they also, given the opportunity, want to *work* for school change. I gradually had student co-investigators in the research and change effort. This collaboration was part of an intervention that moved them from solely blaming themselves when they struggled to also asking about the larger institution's part in their lack of success.

Originally, I had the vision of gathering the student narratives and reporting them back to the school. I thought that when faculty and administrators heard the power and pain of the stories, they would be moved to interrogate school practices that may be alienating to some of the students. What I hadn't anticipated was that *as students heard each other*, they were moved to interrogate school practices they found to be exclusive or alienating. The telling and gathering of stories was a powerful process in terms of creating a collective lens on their struggles in the school. Through this process of ongoing storytelling and analysis, we became partners and collaborators in the research and change processes.

POTENTIAL OF TEACHER ACTION RESEARCH

When I began my research, I took what I think of now as a "flying by the seat of my pants" approach. I was not aware of much in the educational literature that would help guide me as I made my way in what proved to be a complex research process. The 1990s saw a growing literature on teacher research. This literature included academic writing about the process and the issues involved (Anderson & Herr, 1999; Cochran-Smith & Lytle, 1993; Burnaford, Fischer, & Hobson, 1996; Hubbard & Power, 1999) but it also included teacher researchers writing about their work for a larger audience, beyond their own sites of practice (see e.g., *The Practitioner Inquiry Series*, edited by Cochran-Smith & Lytle; Gallas, 1997; Meier, 1997). From these accounts, teachers can learn more about the "how to" of the teacher action research process and what educators learned as they studied their own practices and school sites.

Teacher research is often framed as a valuable way to improve one's own practice (Newkirk, 1992), yet it can also be a tool for larger, schoolwide change (Anderson, Herr, & Nihlen, 1994). Part of the larger category of action research, it implies posing a question about our own practices or about practices taking place in our own worksites. Often, these questions reflect puzzles we, as teachers, are having in our work or concerns we have about the site itself. Typically, we begin to gather data that would help shed light on these puzzles or concerns, with an eye toward devising improved practices. Meaning making of our data begins immediately, as does the problem-solving process.

As we devise interventions or plans to improve our practices, we commit to continue gathering data. Typically, our attempts at improving practices reflect a partial understanding, so the improvements we devise will not be "perfect." We continue to gather data, asking what parts of the intervention we got "right" and where improvements are still needed. This process is often referred to as the *action research spiral*. The continued inquiry is designed to deepen our understanding of the issues involved and construct complex interventions to honor that understanding.

Indeed, some of the hallmarks of "valid" teacher research include areas such as: 1) *process validity*, or the extent that problems are framed and solved in a manner that permits ongoing learning on the part of the individual and/or the larger system; 2) *outcome validity*, or the extent to which actions occur that lead to a "solution" or improvement in the problem that led to the study in the first place; 3) *democratic validity*, or the extent to which research is done in collaboration with various stakeholders or with the goal of trying to tap multiple perspectives; and 4) *catalytic validity*, or the idea that the research should reorient and energize participants toward knowing reality in order to transform it (see Anderson & Herr, 1999, for a fuller discussion of these areas).

Teacher researchers often begin their research with quite practical concerns involving issues of discipline or specific instructional strategies, seeking answers to "what works best." Although some problems of practice may be able to be addressed without recourse to the spiral of inquiry described previously, teacher research done with the criteria of validity spelled out previously will tend to move beyond the isolated resolution of practical problems. My own assumption is that, although I often embark on research that is derived explicitly from the puzzles I encounter in my own practices as an educator, any issue that I research is embedded in the larger life of the school. I believe there is a dynamic interplay between what I do within the confines of my own classroom or my counseling office and what transpires in the larger school context. Because of this interplay, I would suggest that teacher research often has a "spillover" effect; I think that there is something about merely asking certain questions within the context of a school that sends a ripple through it and begins to interrupt the way everyday practices are viewed.

As teacher researchers, we can embrace this ripple and see our inquiry not only as a way to change our own perspectives but also as a part of a larger change process. In my own research, I was concerned about the students who were struggling in my school, but I was not privy initially to the narratives they had to tell about their experiences in the school. In the process of gathering the students' stories, I heard the discourse of the school in a new way. For example, "official" talk in the school was that we were an institution where diverse students could thrive, yet I saw little action to back up that claim.

Like all good action research, the process itself was catalytic in that it reoriented and reframed for me the issue or problem I was trying to tackle. In this case, I moved from more individual work with struggling students to a broader focus. Although I retained my commitment to individual students, I realized that one of the best ways to support students might be to work in the larger school context on issues of institutional prejudice. We, as teachers, are often reflective, mulling over the issues that arise in any given day. I think that taking a step beyond the daily occurrences to systematically look at broader patterns that may affect our practices can yield insights.

Schools are hierarchical places where teachers and students are not necessarily seen as natural allies in either the learning or change processes. In my study, I found that the research process worked to flatten the hierarchical line between students and teachers. We had a common issue on which to work together, from varying positions within the school, but toward a common end.

This flattening is not, of course, without its complexities. Teachers are adults who are employed by the setting they are studying and perhaps critiquing. Students are not typically privy to "adult talk" in schools, and it is assumed that teachers will maintain these hierarchical lines. Adults are often expected to withhold information from students regarding the inner workings of the school and decisions that are made "for the students' good" but without the students' input or perspective. As adults in professional roles, teachers should remain authentic to themselves and to their students and not collude in protecting institutional practices that should be interrogated.

As demonstrated by the stories presented in this book, the way things are ordinarily done may or may not be in the best interests of students. For this reason, teacher researchers are advised to include students (and perhaps their parents and other community members) in their research whenever possible. As teachers, we need to be willing to submit our own cherished beliefs—even "progressive" ones—to examination when the struggles and realities of our students call them into question.

In my research, I could have encouraged the students to adapt to the school environment; in essence, I could have told them to "Put up with it; this is a great opportunity." Instead, the school community decided to try to create a space for the students to rename their experiences, from that of "individual failure" to include problems in the school at large. The former would have reproduced the status quo that was negative for them in the first place; the latter threw all of the staff members into a deconstructing of the school's discourse and the ways it saw itself as a welcoming place for diverse students.

Although challenging the status quo felt risky for us as professionals, it was nothing compared to the risk the students took in offering their critiques, experiences, thoughts, and feelings of how their school might better meet their needs. In light of their courage, we can only offer the same.

REFERENCES

Anderson, G.L., & Herr, K. (1999). The new paradigm wards: Is there room for rigorous practitioner knowledge in schools and universities? *Educational Researcher, 28*(5), 12–21, 40.

Anderson, G.L., Herr, K., & Nihlen, A.S. (1994). *Studying your own school: An educator's guide to qualitative practitioner research.* Thousand Oaks, CA: Corwin Press.

Burnaford, G., Fischer, J., & Hobson, D. (Eds.). (1996). *Teachers doing research practical possibilities.* Mahwah, NJ: Lawrence Erlbaum Associates.

Cochran-Smith, M., & Lytle, S.L. (1993). *Inside outside: Teacher research and knowledge.* New York: Teachers College Press.

Gallas, K. (1997). *Sometimes I can be anything: Power, gender, and identity in a primary classroom.* New York: Teaches College Record.

Hubbard, R.S., & Power, B.M. (1999). *Living the questions: A guide for teacher-researchers.* York, ME: Stenhouse Publishers.

Meier, D.R. (1997). *Learning in small moments: Life in an urban classroom.* New York: Teachers College Press.

Newkirk, T. (1992). *Workshop by and for teachers: The teacher as researcher.* Portsmouth, NH: Heinemann.

Wasley, P.A., Hampel, R.L., & Clark, R.W. (1997). *Kids and school reform.* San Francisco: Jossey-Bass.

28

What's Next for These Youth?

Ginger Blalock

As readers can surmise from the prior chapters in this book, youth with disabilities experience numerous challenges, and hopefully various supports, in their quest to seek or solidify identity, understand their world, complete high school, and face adult demands. Adolescence in itself brings many of those issues, so some of the struggles are universal, such as seeking one's independence and voice, having input into educational decision making, and gaining acceptance among peers. An additional challenge faced by ALL youth is the need to chart a path for the future, one that has significant support in the requirement of the Individuals with Disabilities Education Improvement Act (IDEA) of 2004 (PL 108-446) for transition planning in individualized education programs (IEPs).

In addition to specific disability issues, youth with disabilities are sometimes subject to particular institutional or systemic challenges that present even more barriers. For example, when youth who have been convicted of a crime (a large percentage of whom have identified disabilities) try to return to high school after serving their time, they frequently are blocked from enrolling by school administrators; if they do enroll, few supports exist to help them succeed in completing their high school education. Similarly, youth in foster care (who frequently have medical or other issues) often "age out" of that system and, in some states, find themselves suddenly without income and medical support and with few connections to adult services on their eighteenth birthdays.

A major barrier to fully utilizing the support of IDEA 2004's transition requirements and realizing the potential of such planning is the lack of understanding among students, families, and educators about what transition is and can be and what their respective roles in the planning process should be. The following section provides a short description of transition to set the stage for strategies that have shown promise in recent years.

BRIEF EXPLANATION OF TRANSITION

The term *transition*, in general, can be thought of a movement from one stage in life to another. Historical evidence from statewide and national follow-up studies has shown that transition by design, not by accident, helps youth reach adulthood with a solid direction and the right connections to pursue their chosen paths (Sitlington, Frank, & Carson, 1992; Wagner, Blackorby, Cameto, Hebbeler, & Newman, 1993). Patton and Dunn (1995) portrayed the components that comprise such thoughtful passages in a model (see Figure 28.1), with *student-initiated activities* a key part. Patton and Dunn's model stresses the global aspects of successful movement into adulthood, complemented by the adult outcome areas specified by IDEA 2004 (which can be thought of as postschool goals or strategies). IDEA 2004 states that transition planning, which aims to identify and secure critical transition services, is essential for all students with IEPs by their fourteenth birthdays (or earlier if appropriate).

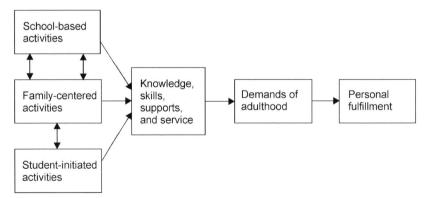

Figure 28.1.   Elements of the transition process. (From Patton, J.R., & Dunn, C. [1995]. *Transition from school to young adulthood: Basic concepts and recommended practices* [p. 5]. Austin, TX: PRO-ED; adapted by permission.)

Transition services are defined in the regulations for IDEA 1997 as:

A coordinated set of activities for a child with a disability that—
(1) Is designed to be within a results-oriented process, that is focused on improving the academic and functional achievement of the child with a disability to facilitate the child's movement from school to post-school activities, including postsecondary education, vocational education, integrated employment (including supported employment), continuing and adult education, adult services, independent living, or community participation. (C.F.R. § 300.42)

Key phrases within the definition include 1) *coordinated set of activities*, which denotes a cohesive package of services, supports, and programs that work well together toward a common aim; 2) *promotes movement from school to post-school activities* which says that the transition plan should help the student achieve his or her own postschool goals; and 3) the list of postschool outcome areas (*postsecondary education* through *community participation*), which reminds educators that this law mandates thoughtful transition planning for *every* student with an IEP, regardless of the student's background, capacities, and long-term vision and prospects. Transition planning helps prepare youth for the full range of major adult life activities listed previously, depending on what the individual envisions for his or her future.

This outcomes-focused planning is not just a map to get to a particular goal but more of a collaborative process that actually connects the student with life after school. Ed O'Leary, educational consultant with Mountain Plains Regional Resource Center and a consulting partner for more than 30 states, often describes an effective transition process as one in which the baton is passed off in a relay race, in contrast to less-helpful approaches where the football is passed down the field in hopes that someone will catch it (O'Leary, 2000). Central to this design is *the student's voice:* IDEA 2004 requires that the decision making in transition planning "be based on student's goals, preferences, and interests" and that the student be invited to the meeting. Students who are 14 or 15 may only need 1) an expression of future goals (e.g., a long-term vision statement) to guide all further discussion, and 2) a course of study for high school (i.e., statement of transition service needs). Students 16 and older also need a 3- to 5-year adult life plan that specifies the strategies to be used over time to help the student reach his or her long-term goals (i.e., statement of needed transition services).

Kohler's (1996) Transition Taxonomy (see Figure 28.2) is a field-validated model of a comprehensive transition program that helps

Figure 28.2.   Taxonomy for transition programming. (*Key:* *collaborative framework or service delivery.)
(From Kohler, P. [1996]. *A taxonomy for transition programming: Linking research and practice* [p. 3].
Champaign: University of Illinois, Transition Research Institute; reprinted by permission.)

one envision where and why students' leadership must occur. The five major facets of a quality transition program are student-focused planning, student development, family involvement in transition, interagency collaboration, and program structures and attributes. Student voice is most critical in student-focused planning, during which student-led IEPs and full student participation in all educational and futures planning should occur. At minimum, students of any age can participate in the goal-setting part of IEP development.

Many students, however, are not sure of their postschool goals (e.g., younger teens will often respond with "I don't know" when asked about their future) or often express goals viewed as unrealistic (e.g., football star, wrestler, rock star). These orientations are not limited to youth with IEPs. These responses provide the IEP team with information—for instance, they suggest that the student needs appropriate career assessment and a career exploration program in order to have something to say or to learn about training and employment opportunities in certain fields.

Student voice is also central in student development, during which youth participate in comprehensive assessment efforts that help describe their status across academic and life domains. Ideally, they learn and apply skills that allow them to be full members of the IEP team and other planning efforts (see next section). In addition, the remaining student development areas are important for success in both current and future settings (academic/content skills, self-determination skills, career exploration and education, career decision making, and generic employability skills).

Educators, parents, and students have much more to learn about the transition process so that they can realize their potential roles in this long-term decision making; fortunately, numerous resources exist. The National Dissemination Center for Children with Disabilities web site (http://www.nichcy.org) offers information that is extremely helpful in supporting students as they take charge of their own planning. It offers links to resources that 1) explain how to design IEP transition plans, 2) clarify IDEA 2004 transition issues, 3) list transition requirements, 4) describe how to involve all community resources in the transition process, and 5) reveal how to encourage students to participate in their own plans.

IMPORTANT FACETS OF
TRANSITION PLANNING FOR YOUTH

For many years after transition requirements were initiated in the law in 1990, IEP teams frequently waived (with minimal justification) or inadequately addressed transition planning for certain categories of students. For example, youth with learning disabilities often were perceived to be functioning well enough to not need transition plans beyond postsecondary education. Students with emotional or behavioral disorders were believed to have more pressing issues in their educational planning, and gifted students who were served in special education were thought to not need transition assistance. Thus, numerous opportunities for thoughtful life planning were missed, and many students became the statistics that cause heartache among parents, educators, and adult services staff (e.g., incarcerated or awaiting adjudication, abusing substances, unemployed or severely underemployed, dependent on family or other caregivers, in dire need of mental health services).

For example, the National Longitudinal Transition Study (http://www.nlts2.org/) reported that 3–5 years postschool, the arrest rate for exiters with disabilities was 56% among dropouts, compared with 16% among graduates and 10% among those who aged out of school. These postschool outcomes are not what students, nor anyone else, want, and transition planning offers beneficial alternatives.

Educators need to ask students what they want from transition planning in order to avoid scenarios such as the one experienced by Jake, as discussed by Clark and Davis. "Because all efforts had been invested in getting him through school, Jake was unprepared to work or to live on his own" (2000, p. 19).

The aspects of transition planning that are *particularly linked to learning what students want* include self-determination, broad assessment, employability skills, career exploration and decision making, and quality-of-life issues. These features, in turn, help get young adults where they want and need to be—in postsecondary education and training, employment, community participation, and/ or the other facets of having a full, satisfying life. Following is an elaboration of students' perspectives of and roles in these key areas.

Self-Determination Skills

Many barriers exist to students' acquisition and/or practice of the basic skills that Martin, Huber-Marshall, Maxson, and Jerman (1997–2000), among others, have associated with self-determination—self-awareness, self-advocacy self-efficacy, decision making, independent performance, self-evaluation, and adjustment. For example, traditional families in some cultures may strongly discourage their youth from disclosing their disabilities in higher education, feeling that their ethnic differences carry enough stigma in some settings without adding more. Those young adults would not likely consider disobeying their elders, even if they felt that they needed support services (Hildreth Combes, 2004). In addition, many school cultures do not truly support student leadership and self-advocacy, thus presenting subtle but daunting roadblocks to students' opportunities to rehearse and refine their self-determination skills.

Jamie Van Dycke, doctoral candidate at the University of Oklahoma, interviewed numerous students with disabilities in her state to learn their perceptions regarding school, special education, and IEPs. The following remarks from students remind educators how essential self-determination skill development is from an early age, including active involvement in the IEP process:

> When should students start going to IEPs? Like I told you, third grade. If it's not too late. Maybe sooner. Maybe second grade for some students. (2003, p. 13)

> Students shouldn't go to a whole meeting all at once! Start off in elementary school, with just finding out who is there and what the meeting is for. Just stay for that part. (2003, p. 15)

My best advice for becoming a self-advocate? It is so hard to talk about your disability. I still get embarrassed. But you get a little more used to it. Friends are the hardest. If you can tell your friends, you can tell anybody. (2003, p. 18)

These comments, like the stories told throughout this book, convey the hardships experienced by these students, as well as the hope they continue to hold for improving their opportunities and acceptance.

Numerous curricula exist for helping preadolescents and adolescents acquire self-determination skills, and some of them particularly focus on preparing students to actively participate in their IEP meetings. The most widely used curricula, in alphabetical order, are listed in Table 28.1. All are easy to understand and require minimal training in order to implement and to evaluate their success. Teachers, students, and parents who use these curricula and allow students to apply these skills in educational planning consistently describe a transformed process in IEP meetings and avow not to return to traditional procedures; holding IEP meetings that are student-centered can be compelling!

Assessment

Several domains of assessment are relevant for transition planning and allow students to know and use findings about themselves in very proactive ways. Academic performance levels are typically available from school and statewide mandated tests and course grades and simply need to be gathered; however, teachers and evaluators need to adequately share results with students as a way to enhance ownership of their learning. Career-related interest and aptitude assessments are common, with annual interest assessment

Table 28.1.   Widely used self-determination curricula in the United States

Field, S., & Hoffman, A. (1996). *Steps to self-determination.* Austin, TX: PRO-ED.

Halpern, A.S., Herr, C.M., Doren, B., & Wolf, N.H. (2000). *Next S.T.E.P.: Student transition and educational planning* (2nd ed.). Austin, TX: PRO-ED.

Martin, J.E., Huber-Marshall, L., Maxson, L., Jerman, P., Hughes, W., & Miller, T. (1997–2000). *ChoiceMaker curriculum.* Longmont, CO: Sopris West.

McGahee, M., Mason, C., Wallace, T., & Jones, B. (2001). *Student-led IEPs: A guide for student involvement.* Arlington, VA: Council for Exceptional Children.

Serna, L.A., & Lau-Smith, J.A. (1995). *Teaching with a PURPOSE: Lesson plan manual for teaching self-determination skills to students who are at-risk for failure.* Manoa: University of Hawaii, Department of Special Education and Hawaii University Affiliated Programs.

Van Reusen, A., Bos, C.S., Schumaker, J.B., & Deshler, D.D. (1994). *Self-advocacy strategy for education and transition planning.* Lawrence, KS: Edge Enterprises.

being the most important for students to understand, learn from, and use in their career planning. Work-related values inventories provide individuals with greater understanding about the features of work that are likely to be most satisfying or irritating to them. Learning styles inventories are often helpful as youth prepare for postsecondary education and learn to request appropriate accommodations. Helpful principles in this support area of assessment are:

- Inform youth about every type of assessment considered, the benefits of doing the assessments, and the possible uses for their results; then let them decide on an individual basis which ones to select and for what purposes.

- Inform each youth privately about the results of all assessment procedures and jointly discuss ways to use the results in educational and transition planning.

- Include all key partners—family members, educators, employers, and related-services staff (e.g., therapists, corrections officers)—in the assessment process; gather information and affirm that the right questions are being asked.

- Ask the youth to design a long-term assessment plan that strategically provides information about him- or herself at critical junctures in his or her schooling.

Employability Skills

The employability skills domain consists of the key competencies that employers identify as essential for productive workers and that are important for *every* individual to be successful. The Secretary's Commission on Achieving Necessary Skills (Kane, Berryman, Goslin, & Meltzer, 1990) competencies comprise the most widely known taxonomy of these skill areas:

- *Resources*—Identifies, organizes, plans, and allocates resources (time, money, materials, facilities, human)

- *Interpersonal*—Works with others (team members, customers, others from diverse backgrounds)

- *Information*—Acquires, organizes, interprets, and evaluates information

- *Systems*—Understands complex interrelationships (in social, organizational, and technological systems)

- *Technology*—Works with a variety of technologies.

Every student can relate to some aspect of these competencies and see their connection to adult life activities at home, school, work, and community. See http://www.doleta.gov for a description of these essential competencies.

Career Exploration

Learning experiences that allow students to explore careers of interest to them comprise one of the foundation elements that help students state future goals. One of our school system's shortcomings has been failure to systematically integrate curricular offerings throughout kindergarten through twelfth-grade education that help students learn specifically of the wide range of options for careers that can help them actualize their dreams for the future. Students with disabilities often need explicit instruction in order to learn some areas of knowledge—in this case, the potential choices they have among the array of broad career clusters that exist in the United States and elsewhere, as well as samplings of specific occupations that fall in those clusters. Educators do not necessarily need to know all of these clusters and occupations, but they do need to know how to get information regarding those careers to students. Follow-up studies have indicated that having a paid job while in high school is one of the strongest predictors of postschool employment success as well as a factor supporting school completion affirming that all students should take advantage of the safety net offered by work study, cooperative education, and similar programs (Blalock, Mahoney, & Van Dyke, 1992; see also http://www.sri.com/policy/cehs/nlts/nltssum.html).

Career Decision Making

Work-based learning experiences can certainly help adolescents decide about career directions. In addition, a small amount of career guidance and counseling fills in the gaps, and numerous resources, from electronic to human, exist to help with selecting various paths to the future. Computer software and web-based programs (e.g., *Choices, Discover, PathFinder*) can help provide critical career information in a branching format while helping the student assess strengths and interests and gradually narrow down choices. The transition specialist or school or college counselor can facilitate successful transitions from high school to postsecondary education or training by informing youth about available programs in their interest areas at selected institutions, providing applications and sample letters, and sharing tips for successful admissions procedures. The sponsor teacher, whether special or general education, or transition specialist can ensure that the youth has completed interest assessments, transition plans, and formal career decision-making instruments that all assist him or her to pinpoint likely career directions.

Agency Supports and Quality-of-Life Issues

Connecting with adult agencies and postsecondary institutions who can provide critical long- or short-term support is a major student need, typically aided by school personnel or case managers during the transition planning process. These connections must be made long before the day of exit from secondary schooling. Staff in those agencies and institutions do their best to help, but their resources are generally much more limited than kindergarten through twelfth-grade education, and thus they require individuals to meet eligibility requirements in order to serve them.

Although these adult agency staff will have difficulty attending every senior IEP meeting, they will meet and collaborate in other ways that make sense (e.g., regular application sessions at the school, annual presentations to families and educators, annual college or career fairs). The postsecondary education special services counselor can assist young adults with disabilities recognized by the Vocational Rehabilitation Act of 1963 (PL 88-210) or the Americans with Disabilities Act of 1990 (PL 101-336) to obtain the accommodations needed to succeed in their chosen fields of study. The adult services case manager and local providers can help qualifying individuals with financial, medical, community access, vocational, and independent living goals and supports to reduce barriers to a smooth adult adjustment.

One young adult interviewed by Clark and Davis (2000) had this advice for support staff:

> I feel it is very important that services fit the person they are intended to help. It is also important for service providers to remember that if they are making an effort to tailor services to a specific young person, they don't give up when the kid has a bad day or is in a bad mood. (2000, p. 81)

SUMMARY

Youth with disabilities have numerous paths from which to choose in order to reach their visions for the future. Smooth transitions out of secondary schooling into the adult world can be guaranteed only if key team members work together to create the plan and provide the services, supports, and programs needed. Of greatest importance is that the individual has a long-term goal and that he or she shares that vision with the support team. The team's responsibility is to ensure that youth develop the understanding to create their visions and that they have the opportunity to express those visions throughout the years in which transition planning occurs. Although it is challenging for adults to relinquish some control, adolescents need the chance to take charge of their educational and transition planning as early as possible so that they can live up to society's expectations to make positive, informed decisions throughout their adult lives.

REFERENCES

Americans with Disabilities Act of 1990, PL 101-336, 42 U.S.C. §§ 12101 *et seq.*

Blalock, G., Mahoney, B., & Van Dyke, R. (1992). *The impact of follow up studies on an urban district and the surrounding state.* Unpublished manuscript, University of New Mexico.

Clark, H.B., & Davis, M. (2000). *Systems of care for children's mental health series: Transition to adulthood: A resource for assisting young people with emotional or behavioral difficulties.* Baltimore: Paul H. Brookes Publishing Co.

Hildreth Combes, B. (2004, October 8). *African American college students with learning disabilities: Their stories, their experiences.* Presentation to the Council for Learning Disabilities International Conference, Las Vegas, NV.

Individuals with Disabilities Education Improvement Act of 2004, PL 108-446, 20 U.S.C. §§ 1400 *et seq.*

Kane, M., Berryman, S., Goslin, D., & Meltzer, A. (1990, September 14). *Secretary's Commission on Achieving Necessary Skills: Identifying and describing the skills required by work.* Washington, DC: U.S. Department of Labor.

Kohler, P. (1996). *A taxonomy for transition programming: Linking research and practice.* Champaign: University of Illinois, Transition Research Institute.

Martin, J.E., Huber-Marshall, L., Maxson, L., & Jerman, P. (1997–2000). *ChoiceMaker curriculum.* Longmont, CO: Sopris West.

O'Leary, E. (2000, Sept. 30). *IDEA transition requirements.* Presentation to the New Mexico Statewide Transition Coordinating Council, Albuquerque, NM.

Patton, J.R., & Dunn, C. (1995). *Transition from school to young adulthood: Basic concepts and recommended practices.* Austin, TX: PRO-ED.

Sitlington, P., Frank, A., & Carson, R. (1992). Adult adjustment among graduates with mild disabilities. *Exceptional Children, 59,* 221–233.

Van Dycke, J. (2003). *It's not easy.* [PowerPoint slide show]. Available at http://www.ou.edu/zarrow/ItsNotEasy.ppt

Vocational Education Act of 1963, PL 88-210, 20 U.S.C. §§ 35 *et seq.*

Wagner, M., Blackorby, J., Cameto, R., Hebbeler, K., & Newman, L. (1993). *The transition experiences of young people with disabilities: A summary of findings from the National Longitudinal Transition Study of special education students.* Menlo Park, CA: SRI International.

29

Am I in the Wrong Class?

Amanda Funicelli

As a freshman in high school, I knew that one day I had to take a class called communication skills. This is a mandatory class for all sophomores, and I couldn't graduate without taking it. One day, my teacher told us about a new communication skills class that was being offered with two teachers instead of one. It sounded as if it could be fun, so I decided to sign up. I didn't even know what the class was really about, but I figured if I had to take the class to graduate, I might as well try something that sounded a little different. I turned in my registration in the spring and forgot about my choices during summer vacation.

On the first day of tenth grade, I checked my schedule. My first period class was communication skills. I walked into the class, and I was scared. There were students in wheelchairs in there! My first thought was, "Oh my gosh! Am I in the wrong class?" I was sure that this was the wrong class—I was positive I had walked into the wrong room. I whispered to the person next to me and asked if this was really the right class and the right room. Indeed, it was, and I didn't know what to expect now.

The bell rang, and two teachers came into the room. They talked to us and, sure enough, explained that this was the communication skills class. The teachers told us that we were getting the chance to meet new people whom we had never met before. I interpreted that as meaning we were going to work with the special ed. kids in the room. My first thought was, "What's the point in that?" But, I stayed in the class, feeling sure of an easy *A*.

For the first few weeks, I didn't enjoy the class at all. It seemed like a waste of time. I couldn't work with those "other" kids. I was expected to work with kids who were different and who I didn't even know. It was really intimidating for me. The teachers asked me to help other students, but I didn't know how to help them. I mean, this class was scary! I had a girl across from me in a wheelchair who could barely write, a girl to the right of me who did everything with her mouth, a girl to the left whose speech I could hardly understand, and a kid across the room who did not talk but made weird noises and drooled.

Down deep in my heart, I knew I wanted to get involved in this class. I knew I wanted to help, but I didn't have a clue about what to do. What if I offended someone, or did something completely wrong? I had never even seen these kids before I walked into the room. Where had they come from? I watched as a few of my classmates stepped in and offered help to the kids who seemed to need it. When I saw that they could do it, I figured I could do it, too.

Nina was the first friend that I worked with in that class. She had a hard time writing, so I just helped her out. I don't know what her disability is, and actually, I don't care. I just know that she is in a wheelchair and needed my help to get her work done. After working with Nina, I felt more comfortable working with some other girls in the class who needed help in reading and writing. I began to realize that it was all kind of easy. These girls were more like me than different from me. I began to feel more at ease.

About a month into the school year, our class went on a field trip to the State Fair. It was during this outing that I really got to know the members of our class. Now, as I look back on my first days in the class, I think it's sad that I felt so awkward working with kids with disabilities. They are high school students just like all the other students in school with me. I guess that it felt weird to me at first because I had never seen any students with disabilities at our school before.

The class became part of my daily routine, and the kids in wheelchairs did not scare me anymore. In fact, this class had a really powerful effect on me. Through this communication skills class, I have made a lot of new friends. I met many people that I never would have even seen if I had not registered for a "different" communication skills class. Before I was part of this class, I looked at kids with disabilities differently. Now, I realize that we are all different—unique—and also all the same.

There is really no reason why the school should keep us separated. If the schools had not kept the general education students apart from the special education students for all of our lives, it wouldn't be so awkward to meet each other and work together. It would just be automatic and natural, as it is for me and everyone else in that class now. For example, when I see people in wheelchairs, I don't avoid eye contact as I used to do. I just smile at them as I do to everyone else.

Most students in schools see students with disabilities the way I used to. If I see or hear someone making fun of someone with a disability, I become angry. I think people just don't understand because they've been separated since elementary school from people who are different in appearance or ability. I think most of the students just don't know how to act around kids with disabilities.

I think that if we would have all been in classes together since we were little that it would have been different. It seems that the little kids are more oblivious of the disabilities of others. I noticed this when we worked on one or our communication skills projects, exchanging letters with our pen pals from the local elementary school. All of the little second graders worshipped all of us sophomores, whether we had a disability or not. We took a field trip and met them at a park. We all played Red Rover, and it was awesome to see how we had all become friends.

This is the reason I believe in inclusion. A few classes may be a little too hard for some kids with disabilities, but there are classes that are too hard for regular ed. kids, too. There are lots of classes that would be perfectly fine for all of us. I don't see anything wrong with regular ed. kids taking a little time to help out the students who really need it. My experience with inclusion has impacted me in many ways that I never could have imagined before. It has been an amazing learning experience for everyone involved. We have learned how to work together and that there are many different kinds of people, but that we are all just people.

Before I took this class, I had no idea what career path I wanted to pursue. Part of our work in the class was to complete a career project. I investigated teaching and became sincerely interested in special education. I realized that, despite my fears at the beginning, I work well with kids who have difficult challenges.

My experiences and the friends I have met have really affected me. Mostly, I have been inspired to be a teacher and to work with kids with disabilities. They need to be in classes with everyone else, and I really want to make that happen for them. I am thankful for the opportunities I have had. I have had the chance to be interviewed for a documentary about inclusion. I have also been part of presentations to new teachers and student teachers during the summer. I've enjoyed sharing my experiences. I have met many people as a result of this communication skills class, and I have discovered my true passion. I look forward to attending the University of New Mexico and earning a dual license in general and special education. And to think that on day one I thought I had entered the wrong class!

30

The Ultimate Goal

Kelsey Holmes

I had never heard of inclusion until I arrived in communication skills my sophomore year of high school. I soon found out how incredibly important it is to both students and people in general. I have learned so much about these wonderfully unique students in my class, and I believe that it is important for everyone to realize what inclusion is and its importance to society.

For almost half a year, I have participated in an inclusive communication skills course. I never previously had students with disabilities in my classes before, and this was a new experience. I was a little hesitant when the school year began, but as the year progressed and I started friendships with these students, I realized they have the same needs for acceptance and friendships.

Inclusion is so important because all people deserve to experience life to the fullest. Students with disabilities cannot achieve this unless they are introduced to society. When you are a teenager, high school is the only true society we know ... it's the only society they know. By accepting them, maybe we can start a new era where the real world values people with disabilities as much as the members of my communication skills class does.

Though this experience has been a great one, it has not always been easy. There have been days where working with the students with disabilities has been trying. However, this is not an excuse to not include them. My advice is to look past the outward actions and remember that one day maybe my patience will help these students live full, productive lives when they graduate.

I believe that all kids have the right to belong, and it is disheartening that even though the number of handicapped students in mainstream education is increasing, society is still not prepared to treat them on an equal basis. When people are not involved or educated about inclusion, this is when they use derogatory and hurtful names for these students. This needs to stop. The only way it will stop is if other students get the opportunities to meet and accept people who are different, and this needs to begin in the schools, not after we have graduated.

I have learned so much about inclusion and have an optimistic attitude that it is the ultimate goal, and each day we are gaining ground toward inclusion in the areas of education and society.

31

Imagine the Possibilities

Frances R. Duff,
Elizabeth B. Keefe, and Veronica M. Moore

We believe that the possibilities that emerge by listening to student voices are virtually limitless. Students' stories present significant implications to the ways in which meaningful curriculums and related services are provided to all children. As educators, it is important that we establish teaching methods, environments, and attitudes that are conducive to learning. Unfortunately, there are often discrepancies between what teachers and students believe are the necessary elements that comprise a valuable educational experience.

Our chapter contributors demonstrate the critical need to consider the studentsí experiences and incorporate their input when setting up school communities where all of the members feel safe, challenged, and welcomed. The students inform us that focusing solely on the "3 Rs" is not enough. They want teachers who treat students as individuals with hopes and dreams, rather than as products of an educational assembly line. In addition to preparing them for postsecondary education or career paths, teachers should create a climate in which justice, compassion, and equity can flourish. Therefore, it is crucial that teachers remain vigilant in the current political climate of school accountability to assure that our schools do not become devoid of humanity in a quest for academic excellence.

The students' message is clear: *All students need to feel as if they belong in the school community.* Unfortunately, segregated

classes abound in otherwise progressive school environments. In countless schools whose mission statements declare the desire to prepare lifelong learners, entire segments of the student population are not being invited to participate. These students are relegated to learning about life from the outskirts of their school communities. Our teenage contributors to this book have given us good reason to rethink the vision of equity in our schools. They remind us repeatedly that the mandates of *Brown v. Board of Education* (1954) are not yet a reality in all of our schools. They have shown us, through their own experiences, that separate cannot be equal.

The Individuals with Disabilities Education Act (IDEA) Amendments of 1997 (PL 105-17) were created to provide much-needed educational opportunities for students with disabilities. One of the unintended consequences has been that sometimes well-meaning teachers and administrators make decisions based on labels without realizing the potential damage they inflict in the interest of protection. By allowing all children the "dignity of risk" (Perske, 1972), a new world of possibilities can open up for students who have been separated from, unchallenged by, and previously unwelcome to the world of the typical high schooler.

Imagine the possibilities if educators provide situations in their classrooms and schools that promote the same degree of acceptance of all of the students. To paraphrase George Bernard Shaw, teachers tend to see things the way they are and ask, "Why?" Students dream of the possibilities and ask "Why not?" We would like to challenge you to echo the question of students, to look at schools from a new point of view—theirs. We ask you to confront tradition and open the door to students' suggestions. See the possibilities that emerge when student voices are added to the educational conversation.

We are grateful to all of the students who have contributed chapters to this book. From their spirits, we have to learned to recognize a truth asserted by Antoine de Saint Exupery in *The Little Prince*, "Grownups never understand anything by themselves" (1943, p. 4). However, our gratitude extends further. We thank them sincerely for the lessons they have taught us. They have enlightened and inspired us. Their voices will be heard in our research and practice for the remainder of our careers. They are the true experts and have changed our views on the extraordinary power teachers can have on the lives of their students. We have learned to listen, how to trust, and how to let go. Now, it's your turn.

REFERENCES

Brown v. Board of Education, 347 U.S. 483 (1954).

Individuals with Disabilities Education Act (IDEA) Amendments of 1997, PL 105-17, 20 U.S.C. §§ 1400 *et seq.*

Perske, R. (1972). The dignity of risk. In W. Wolfensberger (Ed.), *The principle of normalization in human services* (pp. 194–200). Toronto: National Institute on Mental Retardation.

Saint Exupéry, A. (1943). *The little prince.* New York: Harcourt.

Index

Page numbers followed by *f* indicate figures;
those followed by *t* indicate tables.